Facsimile Edition with introduction by Irving Lowens

KENTUCKY HARMONY

OR

*A CHOICE COLLECTION OF PSALM TUNES,
HYMNS, AND ANTHEMS.*

IN THREE PARTS.

SELECTED BY

A. DAVISSON.

1816.

Augsburg Publishing House • Minneapolis

KENTUCKY HARMONY

Facsimile Edition

Introduction by Irving Lowens
Copyright © 1976 Augsburg Publishing House
All rights reserved.

ISBN 0-8066-1546-X

For the convenience of the user of this facsimile edition,
new page numbers have been placed in the lower outside margins
and a new index using these numbers is on pages 15-16.
The original page numbers still appear and are used in the original index.

This facsimile edition is a photographic reproduction of a copy of the first edition
owned by the Clements Library, University of Michigan, Ann Arbor.

MANUFACTURED IN UNITED STATES OF AMERICA

1 2 3 4 5 6 7 8 9 0 1 2 3 4 5 6 7 8 9 0

INTRODUCTION TO THE FACSIMILE EDITION

There are really very few tune books which deserve to be called landmarks in the history of American music. Certainly, the earliest was the so-called *Bay Psalm Book*, the first book-length product of a printing press in British North America, with its "admonition to the Reader" regarding the tunes in the newly translated metrical version of *The Whole Booke of Psalmes* (1640), which seemingly was added as a space-filler or an afterthought on the final page of the edition.[1] More than half a century passed before we reached another milestone in the form of the ninth (1698) edition of the *Bay Psalm Book* which contained an 11-page supplement in musical notation printed crudely from wood blocks "with the Bass set under each Tune" and a syllabic notation using the letters F, S, L, and M for *fa, sol, la,* and *mi* (then current British practice) placed directly under the notes.[2] The 13 tunes found on these pages represent the first music published in what was later to become the United States.

Another crucially important tune book, assembled by the Rev. John Tufts (1689-1750) and first published in Boston in 1721, was "a small Book containing 20 Psalm Tunes, with Directions how to sing them, contrived in the most easy Method ever yet invented, for the ease of Learners, whereby even Children or People of the meanest Capacities, may come to sing them by Rule."[3] This collection and its "easy Method" (commonly known as *An Introduction to the Singing of Psalm-Tunes*) proved to be a strong weapon in the never-ending American war against musical illiteracy and in the development of a new social institution, the itinerant singing school.[4]

The next significant milestone occurred with the publication in 1770 by Edes and Gill of *The New-England Psalm-Singer: or, American Chorister,* "composed by William Billings, a native of Boston, in New England." It was "the first published compilation of entirely American music; moreover, it was the first tunebook produced by a single American composer."[5] This was, in effect, our musical declaration of independence from Great Britain, and it is interesting that it preceded our political declaration of independence by some six years.

A further giant step forward took place in 1801, when William Little and William Smith, two obscure singing masters, brought out *The Easy Instructor, or A New Method of Teaching Sacred Harmony* in Philadelphia, the first of 34 editions and issues (the last of which appeared in 1831) of a tune book which was to influence profoundly the directions of American music, especially in the South and West, until our own times. Harking back to words very similar to those used by John Tufts, Little and Smith described *The Easy Instructor* and their "New method of teaching Sacred Harmony" as "containing the Rudiments of Music on an improved plan, wherein the naming and timing [of] the notes are familiarized to the weakest capacity." The collection itself was highly eclectic and peculiarly American in content—it was, in effect, a fine anthology of the best that had come out of the New England idiom—but it was the "New method" which was to give it immortality. This consisted in the development of a sight-reading system in which a differently shaped note head was used to represent each of the four syllables then used in solmization. Thus, a triangular note head represented *fa,* an oval note head *sol,* a square note head *la,* and a diamond note head *mi.* In all other respects, the Little and Smith notation was completely orthodox. For comparatively simple music, the advantages of the shape note system are immediately apparent. The distinctive shapes for each syllable enabled anyone, even an illiterate, to name the syllables just about instantaneously, and the identification of scale degrees through shape notes continues even when words rather than the syllables themselves are sung. After a relatively slow start, the Yankee-simple device caught on quickly in rural sections of the country, particularly after a combine of Albany, N.Y., printers began publishing *The Easy Instructor* in 1804.[6]

The Little and Smith shape notes bred imitators and outright pirates, and it was in Harrisburg, Pa., that a printer and amateur musician named John Wyeth, who also published the daily newspaper, *The Oracle of Dauphin,* became convinced of the utility of the new notational system. Charles and George Webster and Daniel Steele of Albany began printing shape notes cast from type in 1808 and Wyeth, seeing a business opportunity, had a font of shape notes cast and in 1810 began printing tune books using them, issuing in that year Joseph Doll's *Leichter Unterricht in der Vokal Musik* (in which even the Little and Smith title was plagiarized),

and an excellent imitation of *The Easy Instructor* entitled the *Repository of Sacred Music.* The latter was enormously successful, and Wyeth had to bring out new editions not only in 1811 and 1812, but many times later.

Then, in 1813, Wyeth (doubtless with the assistance of his music editor, the Rev. Elkanah Kelsay Dare) hit upon something quite new. Using the Little and Smith shapes, he published his *Repository of Sacred Music, Part Second.* Here was combined, for the first time, the vigorous music of the New England singing masters so characteristic of the 1801 *Easy Instructor* and the 1810 *Repository* with what was christened by the late George Pullen Jackson "spiritual folk song," that is, secular folk music of the Anglo-Scottish-Irish persuasion set to religious texts which happened to fit the meter. Spiritual folk song can be traced back in this country nearly a century before it appeared in print in Wyeth's *Repository, Part Second,* but basically as part of an oral tradition. In the *Repository, Part Second,* the music of the written New England tradition and of the oral folk tradition were joined together in print for the first time. Together, the two traditions became one, a hybrid which migrated to the South and the West and later came to be known as Southern folk hymnody.[7] It remains very much alive in isolated parts of the country even today.

Wyeth's *Repository, Part Second* may have been the source from which Southern folk hymnody flowed, but its influence was exerted at second hand through another tune book, Ananias Davisson's compilation entitled *Kentucky Harmony,* printed in 1816 at Harrisonburg, Va., a Shenandoah Valley way station en route to the Kentucky and Tennessee frontier country. It is somewhat ironic that on Feb. 28 of that year, the Albany printers of *The Easy Instructor,* alarmed by the proliferation of tune books making use of their shape note system, were granted a patent covering the casting and use of the shape note types—the patent was awarded to George Webster, acting as agent for his brother, Charles, and Daniel Steele—but by then it was too late to stem the tide of unauthorized publications. Among other Little and Smith shape note books which had appeared before the patent was issued were *Patterson's Church Music* (Cincinnati, 1813; 2nd ed., 1815), Freeman Lewis' *Beauties of Harmony* (Pittsburgh, 1813; 3rd ed., 1818), and Joseph Funk's *Die Allgemein nützliche Choral-Music* (Harrisonburg, Va., 1816; many later editions). Timothy Flint's *Columbian Harmonist* (Cincinnati, 1817), Samuel L. Metcalf's *Kentucky Harmonist* (Cincinnati, 1817), James M. Boyd's *The Virginia Sacred Musical Repository* (Winchester, Va., 1818), Alexander Johnson's *Tennessee Harmony* (Cincinnati, 1818), and Allen D. Carden's *The Missouri Harmony* (St. Louis, 1820; seven later editions in 19 issues)[8] followed soon after. By the time the second (1817) and third (1819) editions of the *Kentucky Harmony* had appeared, Davisson was ready to issue his *Supplement to The Kentucky Harmony* (Harrisonburg, Va., 1820; third ed., Mt. Vernon, Va., 1826?), a quite extraordinary compilation of spiritual folk song much more distinctly oriented in the direction of Southern folk hymnody than the *Kentucky Harmony* itself.

Very little is known about Ananias Davisson's career as a musician except for the publication of his various tune books between 1816 and 1826. He was born in Shenandoah County, Va., on Feb. 2, 1780, and died in Rockingham County, Va., on Oct. 21, 1857, and although he appears to have traveled fairly widely in the "Western country" (a notice in the *Knoxville Register* for May 26, 1818, advises that he will shortly open a singing school using the second edition of the *Kentucky Harmony* as text, and both that tune book and its *Supplement* were sold in Tennessee, Kentucky, North Carolina, South Carolina, Missouri, and Ohio in addition to Virginia), most of his days were spent in the Shenandoah Valley not far from Harrisonburg. From the concrete evidence of Davisson's tune books, it is plain that he must have learned enough about music to read it, write it, teach it, and set it in type before 1816, when the *Kentucky Harmony* first saw the light of day. One student of Southern folk hymnody has postulated a connection between Davisson and members of the Chapin family (no fewer than seven of whom were actively involved in music at the time), and it is quite possible that he attended singing schools taught in Virginia by either Lucius Chapin (1760-1842) or his younger brother, Amzi (1768-1835), both of whom taught music in Virginia in the 1790s. Lucius arrived in the Shenandoah Valley in 1787 and moved to Fleming County, Ky., in 1794. He lived there until 1835, when he emigrated to Hamilton County, Ohio, where he lived for the remainder of his life. If Davisson was, in fact, his pupil (or his apprentice), that might explain why he chose to call his *magnum opus Kentucky Harmony,* an otherwise inexplicable title. It is true that Harrisonburg was a depot on the Valley Turnpike, which connected with the Great Valley Road at Lynchburg, Va., and then (at Abingdon, Va.) joined the Wilderness Road into Kentucky, but it would seem, that a title like *The Virginia Harmony, The Shenandoah Harmony,* or *The Harrisonburg Harmony* would be considerably more appropriate for a valley resident than the one he ultimately selected. Perhaps Davisson figured that the *Kentucky Harmony* would be attractive to the hundreds of families who were traveling the routes southwestward —but this is no more than speculation.

How, where, with whom, and why Davisson learned the printer's trade is another unsolved mystery, but in 1816, at the age of 36, he was in Harrisonburg, Va., working in that capacity. During the course of his 10-year career as a printer[10] (see Table II for a list of his publications), he turned out 15 items, of which 12 were musical in nature and all but one were self-compiled. As he was essentially self-taught in music, so the evidence of his imprints indicates that he was also an autodidact in printing. His tune books are studded with typographical errors, and the reader is advised to use extreme caution in working through Davisson's various tune books. A fairly reliable rule of thumb in reading the music he printed is to trust the shape of the note head rather than its location on the staff where there is a conflict between the two, which is by no means an infrequent state of affairs. Another curious Davisson musical mannerism was his failure to utilize sharps, flats, or naturals—except in the key signature. This gives the Davisson versions of familiar folk hymns a strongly modal aspect, which may or may not have reflected the actual practice of the time and place. In the light of the strongly modal character of the spiritual folk song, it may more accurately reflect what the folk actually were doing than would the transcriptions of more "scientific" musicians better equipped with musical backgrounds. In any event, the lack of accidentals in a Davisson setting is a Davisson trademark, and it can be traced in many later tune books published in the South and West.

Davisson's ability to handle words was no greater, in a technical sense, than his ability to handle musical notation, and his writing is studded with grammatical errors and mistakes in spelling. Only a single document actually in Davisson's handwriting is extant—a letter, written from Knoxville, Tenn., on July 13, 1820, to one Henry Kern of Woodstock in Shenandoah County, Va. "I have thought proper to let you know that I have faild gitting Littles deed as I expected," the letter began, and continued in much the same semi-illiterate vein.[11]

If Davisson's skills as printer, musician, and writer were somewhat limited, he turned out to be an excellent real estate operator and businessman. As a matter of fact, the first mention of his name is in the official records of Rockingham County, where he is listed as having purchased 18¼ acres of land for $316 2/3 on Oct. 15, 1804. He seems to have poured his profits as tune book compiler and publisher into the purchase of land, and of 19 Rockingham County deeds listing him as a grantee, 10 fall within the period of 1818 to 1826. Thereafter, he seems to have augmented his income by a systematic sale of parcels of land, and 10 of the 13 deeds to land acquired by him show that he disposed of them at shrewdly spaced intervals after 1827. Indeed, according to the 1850 census, the value of the real estate he still possessed was estimated at $10,265, a considerable sum of money for the period, and after his death in 1857, his widow's estate was evaluated at $14,000, of which $12,000 was in real estate and $2000 in personal belongings.

Davisson was referred to in the 1820 census as a resident of Harrisonburg owning one male slave aged between 27 and 45 and engaged in "manufacture." On May 7, 1825, he filed a civil suit against Henry Kern (the case was finally settled in Dec., 1829) and on Feb. 24, 1826, less than a year before his retirement from the printing business, he was married. According to the 1840 census, the Davisson household consisted of one free colored male, five male slaves, three female slaves, husband Ananias and wife Ann, and of the 11 household members, six were engaged in "agriculture." Davisson was the defendant in a civil suit filed against him on May 4, 1847, by one John Miller which was dismissed or settled out of court, and in the same year, he was elected one of four trustees of the Union Congregation of the Presbyterian Church in Rockingham County. A staunch Presbyterian all his life, Davisson was buried in the churchyard of the Union Congregation (now called the Massanutten Cross Keys Church), and a headstone marks his final resting place. Although he was a slave owner, as were most prosperous Southerners of the time, there is some evidence that he was not happy with the institution and his will does contain a provision for their manumission. "In consideration of their services to me—and to carry out my intention long entertained I manumit and set free from slavery all my servants," he wrote, "those over the age of eighteen to be free and set at liberty immediately upon my decease; those under that age to serve and labor for my wife until they shall severally reach that age, when and at which time, they are to be free and set at liberty. But if any of my said servants shall refuse to accept their freedom he, she, or they may be sold after choosing a master—and the price to become part of my estate and provided also, that if my woman Sylvia elects to take her freedom, she may take her two youngest children with her to a free state otherwise she shall remain a slave until the youngest child arrives at the age of 18 years." [12]

Davisson's *chef d'oeuvre, Kentucky Harmony,* appeared in no less than five editions between 1816 and 1826. The first edition contains a collection of 143 tunes on pp. 9-138, preceded by 12 pages of rudimentary instructions (an indication of his lack of skill in book makeup) and followed by a two-page index in which the composers of the anthologized tunes are named. Unlike Wyeth, who claimed that 58 of the 149 tunes in his *Repository, Part Second* (1813) were "new," Davisson made no attempt to identify those tunes he was printing for the first time. In point of fact, he did introduce 17 new tunes: seven by himself, five by Capt. R. Boyd, two by Capt. R. Munday, and one each by Josiah Moore, one of the Chapin brothers, and an otherwise unidentified tune-smith named Bozelle. The first edition also contained no less than 57 fuging tunes (only one of which, by Davisson himself, entitled IMMENSITY, was not reprinted from a different source), compared to 31 in Wyeth's *Part Second,* while 32 of Davisson's tunes which can be characterized as folk hymns.

What were the sources of the *Kentucky Harmony?* In the first

7

edition of the tune book, Davisson writes that "from his practical knowledge as a teacher of sacred music, and his extensive acquaintance with most eminent masters, together with the great opportunity which he has had of selecting tunes from the latest and most approved authors in that science," [13] he has gathered his harvest, but he gives us no further clue to its origins. But in the second edition, published only a year later (and unmistakably the same tune book despite a fair number of changes—some tunes were omitted and a considerable number, including seven new tunes by Davisson himself, were added, bringing the total to 148), he is much more explicit. Following the index on page 152, he gives special thanks to "the Gentlemen Teachers in Virginia, Tennessee, and Kentucky" and names Capt. R. Boyd, Capt. Wm. Davidson, Maj. Jno. Martin, Capt. J. Vigar, Capt. R. Monday, and Messrs. Jno. A. Douglass, A. D. Carden, R. D. Humphreys, Jas. J. Wilson, Jno. S. Smith, Jas. C. Lowry, and Jas. Logan as individuals to whom he is particularly indebted (and among whom are undoubtedly some of "the most eminent masters" to whom he had earlier referred). The reader will recognize here the names of some of the composers from whose works Davisson drew. He also—most obligingly—cited the names of Smith, Little, Wyeth, Billings, Holyoke, Atwell, and Peck as compilers of tune books to which he had access in compiling the *Kentucky Harmony*, but unfortunately neglected to give the actual titles. But perhaps these clues will suffice to run down his actual sources.

The reader has already been introduced to *The Easy Instructor* by William Little and William Smith, and no doubt Davisson owned an edition or editions of this popular tune book. By the time the *Kentucky Harmony* first saw the light of day, no less than 16 editions of the Little and Smith compilation had been published, with the contents changing from edition to edition. [14] It is probable that Davisson utilized one of the four 104-page, typographically printed editions issued in Albany, N.Y., between 1809 and 1811; in her 1972 dissertation on Davisson, Rachel Augusta Brett Harley notes that 43% of the tunes in the first edition of the *Kentucky Harmony* may also be found in the 1809 edition of *The Easy Instructor*. Perceptible influence cannot be traced to any tune book by William Billings (even though Davisson did use a fair number of Billings tunes), Samuel Holyoke, Thomas H. Atwill, or Daniel Peck even though these individuals are specifically named. From a study of the contents of the *Kentucky Harmony*, it is evident that Davisson omitted the name of at least one compiler from whose work he borrowed—that of Nehemiah Shumway, whose *American Harmony* was published in Philadelphia in 1793 and reprinted there in 1801. Some 40% of Davisson's tunes may be found there, including a fair number not reprinted elsewhere. Another pair of compilers probably represented in Davisson's library was Andrew Adgate and Ishmael Spicer, who were responsible for *The Philadelphia Harmony*, a point made by Harley.

But the finger of suspicion still points directly at John Wyeth, despite Harley's demonstration that the *Repository, Part Second* was not as important in the genesis of the *Kentucky Harmony* as I claimed it was in 1964 in my introduction to the facsimile edition of the *Repository, Part Second,* where I stated that "a comparative analysis of the Davisson and Wyeth books conclusively demonstrates that *Part Second* was the salient folk-hymnodic influence in the content of the *Kentucky Harmony*." [15] Harley points out that of the 91 previously published tunes in *Part Second,* only 13 may be found in the *Kentucky Harmony,* and of these only five are identical copies, while of the 58 new tunes in the Wyeth tune book, only 17 were used by Davisson, with four identical. The changes made by Davisson in the supposedly "copied" tunes were quite considerable and included the addition of new voice parts, the alteration of others, and in at least five instances, completely new settings in which only the tenor (or melodic line) was retained. In Davisson's hands, the tunes notated earlier in *Part Second* became quite different entities. In the case of the five tunes first published by Wyeth and used, with completely new harmonizations, Davisson (Wyeth's ADORATION= Davisson's CONDESCENSION; GLASGOW; Wyeth's MESSIAH=Davisson's MOUNT CALVARY; Wyeth's NEW CANAAN=Davisson's REFLECTION; Wyeth's KEDRON=Davisson's GARLAND—listed in the index of the first edition of the *Kentucky Harmony* but not printed until the second, its place being taken by GLASGOW), there are conflicting claims of authorship. It is quite evident that Davisson, who claimed to be the "composer" of the setting in each instance, was using the word in the archaic sense of a person "who puts together parts or elements" rather than in the modern sense of a person who invents a piece of music. No piracy was intended by Davisson when he claimed as his own a previously published work; in actual fact, Davisson's new arrangement of the parts entitled him, in the parlance of his day, to claim it as his own composition. Furthermore, the common appearance of 30 items in both *Part Second* and the *Kentucky Harmony* does not bear out my previous claim that the former was the salient influence in shaping the latter. One must take into consideration the influence not only of the *Repository, Part Second* (which is plain, but not conclusive) but also that of Wyeth's *Repository, Part First* (1810), from which Davisson borrowed no less than 68 items. Thus, the two Wyeth *Repositories* account for no less than 98 of the 143 tunes found in Davisson's first tune book. If the 17 tunes Davisson brought out for the first time are subtracted from the total, the Wyeth tune books account for nearly 80% of the tunes found in the *Kentucky Harmony.* It would be difficult to make out a more convincing case for priority of influence.

Despite the Wyeth influence (or the influence of Dare, Wyeth's music editor), the creative aspect of Davisson's work should not be underestimated. Davisson was a conscientious musician with strong ideas about the manner in which a piece of music should sound, and it is rare that he repeats a work *verbatim et literatim.* He was particularly concerned with full four-part harmonizations —in many instances, previously published folk hymns had appeared in two or three parts only—and he was clearly dissatisfied with the pedestrian quality of the alto line, usually the last one written by New England and Southern tunesmiths and thus most frequently the least imaginative. Davisson devoted much care to the problem of making the individual melodic lines accompanying the tune more singable, and he was probably a pioneer in the "Southernizing" process which took place with folk hymns whereby the tunes themselves (as well as the accompanying lines) were notated in the embellished style in which they were undoubtedly frequently performed. Just how different and individualistic a Davisson setting could be is well illustrated in the manner in which he handled KEDRON, claimed in the *Repository, Part Second* as the work of Elkanah Kelsay Dare (but in fact published as early as 1799 in Amos Pilsbury's *The United States' Sacred Harmony*) and "reprinted" in the *Kentucky Harmony* (see illustration, p. 12).

Having established the progression of Southern folk hymnody from Wyeth's two *Repositories* to Davisson's the *Kentucky Harmony*, there is one question which still calls for an answer: How important was this tune book as a wellspring of one of the most significant and interesting American vocal traditions? That question was answered without equivocation by George Pullen Jackson as long ago as 1933, when he wrote in his *White Spirituals in the Southern Uplands:*

"Davisson's ability in selecting for his *Kentucky Harmony* those tunes of other composers which made a deep appeal to his particular public is evinced by the extremely large number of those tunes which became stock-in-trade for the southern rural compilers who followed him. In fact, there are many signs that point to this book and to its *Supplement* as being unique in the wide recognition accorded to them as pioneer repositories of a sort of song that the rural South really liked." [16]

Indeed, it did not take very long for the *Kentucky Harmony* to establish its hegemony in this field. In 1816, the same year Davisson brought out the tune book, Joseph Funk published a German-language tune book in Harrisonburg entitled *Die allgemein nützliche Choral-Music,* a collection of two-part settings printed for him by Laurentz Wartmann. Most of the music used by Funk was borrowed from the song books of the Reformed Church, the Mennonites, and the Lutherans, but the unsuspecting reader comes across a surprise when he reaches page 48, where there are two songs, as Funk acknowledges, "von der Kentuckie Harmonie genommen." These are "Ihr junge Helden, aufgewacht" and "Ach Gott, wie manches Herzeleid," ROCKBRIDGE (p. 9) and SUPPLICATION (p. 12), both by Chapin. Funk also borrowed two additional tunes from the same source but without acknowledgment: "Was mich auf dieser Welt betrübt" (p. 58 in Funk, but Boyd's SALVATION on p. 15 in Davisson) and "Auf, Seele, auf, und säume nicht" (p. 65 in Funk, but Chapin's PRIMROSE on p. 10 in Davisson). This is the earliest instance known to me of the startling mixture of styles, traditions, and languages which later came to characterize a still virtually unknown bilingual tune book literature of mid-nineteenth century Pennsylvania.[17]

Although James P. Carrell's *Songs of Zion* was printed by Davisson in Harrisonburg in 1821 and, as would be reasonable to expect, was strongly influenced by the *Kentucky Harmony,* it is, in fact, surprisingly individualistic. Not so William Moore's *Columbian Harmony* (Cincinnati, 1825), registered for copyright on April 2, 1825, in the District of West Tennessee, despite its Cincinnati imprint. According to Jackson, "the Introduction shows that Moore leaned heavily on Ananias Davisson, [and] in it the

Tennesseean declared that he had followed the Shenandoah musician 'in laying aside several [musical] characters as useless, viz., the accidental sharp and flat, the natural, the hold, the staccato, the direct, and the counter cleff.' And, as to stating reasons for his exclusions, 'Mr. Davisson has done it before me, and my own experience proves to me their inutility.'" Moore also borrowed heavily from Davisson's stock of standard tunes and included no less than 13 attributed to the compiler of *The Kentucky Harmony.*

Other Davisson-influenced tune books of the period included William Caldwell's *Union Harmony* (Maryville, Tenn., 1837), in which 63 of a total of 145 tunes duplicate those in *The Kentucky Harmony* and John B. Jackson's *The Knoxville Harmony of Music Made Easy* (Madisonville, Tenn., 1838), which includes 54 of the *Kentucky Harmony* tunes.[18]

But the major carrier of the Davisson-derived tradition (in the same sense that the *Kentucky Harmony* was the major carrier of the Wyeth-derived tradition) was Allen D. Carden's extraordinarily popular *The Missouri Harmony*, first published in St. Louis (although printed in Cincinnati) in 1820, and last published in Cincinnati in 1858 after a run of 20 separate issues of eight distinct editions, meticulously described in a fine bibliographical study by the late Ernst C. Krohn, pioneer historian of music in midwestern America. According to Krohn, "of the 144 tunes [recte 146] in the second edition of [the *Kentucky Harmony*], Carden included 111 in his compilation. The early masters of singing schools and the compilers of tune books were probably a very cooperative group of men,"[19] he wrote, and he points out that Carden's name is included among the "Gentlemen Teachers in Virginia, Tennessee, and Kentucky" who were helpful to Davisson which appears in the second edition of the *Kentucky Harmony.*

The influence of *The Kentucky Harmony* continued to be felt in the South as late as the appearance of William Walker's *The Southern Harmony* (New Haven, 1835) and the B. F. White and E. J. King *Sacred Harp* (Philadelphia, 1844). An analysis of the 1854 edition of *The Sacred Harp* shows that it utilized 58 tunes chosen by Davisson; the 1860 edition of the *Sacred Harp* used 44.

As I wrote some years ago, "our folk-hymnody is, of course, significant as a written record of the exact state of the American singing tradition in the first half of the nineteenth century, but entirely aside from its historical interest, it is a body of music of great individuality, genuine merit, and melodic charm. It is possibly the most valuable musical heritage that has come down to us from early American times."[20] Ananias Davisson's the *Kentucky Harmony* is one of the most important and influential collections of American folk hymnody ever compiled, and despite its once great popularity, it has become a great rarity. Few have ever been privileged to examine one of the tiny number of extant copies. May this facsimile edition help to bring about a renaissance of interest in the music it contains, as well as commemorate two centuries of this nation's independence.

IRVING LOWENS
Reston, Virginia
January 1, 1976

KEDRON. L M. Flat Key on E.

How pleasant, how divinely fair,
O Lord of hosts, thy dwellings are! With long desire my spirit faints, To rise & dwell among thy saints.

KEDRON. L. M. Minor Key on E.

Thou man of grief, remember me, Thou never canst thyself forget; Thy last expiring agony, Thy fainting pangs and bloody sweat.

Table I

Davisson's *Kentucky Harmony:* A Conspectus of Editions

Edition	Date	Pagination	Locations
1	1816	xii, 9-140 p.	Western Kentucky State University, Bowling Green, Ky.; Clements Library, University of Michigan, Ann Arbor; Grosvenor Reference Division, Buffalo and Erie County Public Library, Buffalo
2	1817	150, 41-44, 151-160 p.	Library of Congress, Washington; Newberry Library, Chicago; University of Kentucky, Lexington; American Antiquarian Society, Worcester; Eastern Mennonite College, Harrisonburg, Va.; University of Virginia, Charlottesville
3	1819	154 p.	University of Kentucky, Lexington (incomplete); Glenn C. Wilcox, Murray, Ky.
4	1821	160 p.	Library of Congress, Washington; Goshen College Biblical Seminary, Goshen, Ind.; American Antiquarian Society, Worcester; University of Tennessee, Knoxville; Virginia State Library, Richmond; Virginia Historical Society, Richmond; Eastern Mennonite College, Harrisonburg, Va.
5	1826	160 p.	Library of Congress, Washington (2); University of Kentucky, Lexington; Massachusetts Historical Society, Boston; Grosvenor Reference Division, Buffalo and Erie County Public Library, Buffalo; Duke University, Durham, N.C.; Madison College, Harrisonburg, Va. (2); University of Virginia, Charlottesville; Virginia Historical Society, Richmond

Table II

Publications from Davisson's Press in Harrisonburg, 1816-26

	Year	Title
1.	1816	The Kentucky Harmony, 1st ed.
2.	1817	The Kentucky Harmony, 2nd ed.
3.	1818	Essays of Conrad Speece
4.	1818	Conrad Speece, The Mountaineer; 2nd ed.
5.	1819	The Kentucky Harmony, 3rd ed.
6.	1820	Supplement to The Kentucky Harmony; 1st ed.
7.	1820	Life and Labors of Rev. Benjamin Abbott (printed for James A. Dillworth)
8.	1821	James P. Carrell, Songs of Zion
9.	1821	The Kentucky Harmony; 4th ed.
10.	1821	An Introduction to Sacred Music
11.	?	Supplement to the Kentucky Harmony; 2nd ed.
12.	1825	A Small Collection of Sacred Music; 1st ed.
13.	1825/26	Supplement to The Kentucky Harmony; 3rd ed. (title-page gives 1825; comments after index dated July, 1826)
14.	1826	The Kentucky Harmony; 5th edition
15.	1826?	A Small Collection of Sacred Music; 2nd ed. (printed at Mt. Vernon, Va.)

FOOTNOTES

1. For details see "The Bay Psalm Book in 17th-Century New England" in Irving Lowens, *Music and Musicians in Early America* (New York, 1964), pp. 28-31.

2. An easily available source of information is Richard G. Appel's *The Music of the Bay Psalm Book, 9th Edition (1698),* I.S.A.M. Monographs, V (Brooklyn, 1975). There is, however, strong evidence of an earlier (1689-91) printing in England of exactly the same music section; for details, *vide* the essay cited in fn. 1, pp. 36-38.

3. *Boston News-Letter,* Jan. 2/9, 1721.

4. The complete story is told in "John Tufts's *Introduction to the Singing of Psalm-Tunes* (1721-1744): The First American Music Textbook" in Lowens, *Music and Musicians,* pp. 39-57. At the time I wrote that essay, the earliest extant edition of Tufts was the 5th (1726); since then, Theodore M. Finney has located a copy of the 3rd (1723) edition in the Warrington Collection housed in the Pittsburgh Theological Seminary and has described it in "The Third Edition of Tufts' *Introduction to the Art of Singing Psalm-Tunes*," *Jour. of Res. in Mus. Ed.* XIV (1966), 163-170.

5. David McKay and Richard Crawford, *William Billings of Boston: Eighteenth-Century Composer* (Princeton, 1975), p. 41.

6. Irving Lowens and Allen P. Britton, "*The Easy Instructor* (1798-1831): A History and Bibliography of the First Shape-Note Tune-Book," in Lowens, *Music and Musicians,* p. 116.

7. *Vide* "John Wyeth's *Repository of Sacred Music, Part Second* (1813): A Northern Precursor of Southern Folk-Hymnody" in Lowens, *Music and Musicians,* pp. 138-140, and my introd. to the facsim. ed. of the *Repository, Part Second* (New York, 1964).

8. Ernst C. Krohn, "A Check List of Editions of *The Missouri Harmony,*" *Bull. of the Mo. Hist. Soc.,* VI (1950), 374-399.

9. Charles Hamm, "The Chapins and Sacred Music in the South and West," *Jour. of Res. in Mus. Ed.,* VIII (1960), 91-98.

10. In the 5th (1826) edition of *The Kentucky Harmony,* Davisson specifies the exact date of his retirement from the printing trade as Nov. 2, 1826.

11. The complete text is given in Rachel Augusta Brett Harley's excellent unpubl. diss. (U. of Mich., 1972), "Ananias Davisson: Southern Tune Book Compiler (1780-1857)," pp. 142-143.

12. Most of the above information about Davisson is derived from the dissertation cited in fn. 11; Davisson's complete will is quoted in its entirety by Harley on pp. 148-149.

13. P. iii.

14. Appendix B (pp. 292-310) in Lowens, *Music and Musicians* contains a checklist of editions and issues as well as an analysis of the constantly changing content of *The Easy Instructor.*

15. Pp. vii-x.

16. Pp. 29-30.

17. The Funk tune book is discussed on pp. 31-34 of Jackson's *White Spirituals* (Chapel Hill, 1933).

18. Jackson, *White Spirituals,* pp. 50-54.

19. Krohn, "*The Missouri Harmony:* A Study in Early American Psalmody," *Bull. of the Mo. Hist. Soc.,* VI (1949), 29.

20. Introd., facsim. ed., Wyeth's *Repository, Part Second,* p. xiv.

INDEX TO THE FACSIMILE EDITION

KENTUCKY HARMONY

OR

A CHOICE COLLECTION OF PSALM TUNES, HYMNS, AND ANTHEMS.

IN THREE PARTS.

TAKEN FROM THE MOST EMINENT AUTHORS, AND WELL ADAPTED TO CHRISTIAN CHURCHES
SINGING SCHOOLS, OR PRIVATE SOCIETIES.

SELECTED BY

A. DAVISSON.

PART I.

1816.

This Book will be sold by the different Book-Sellers, in the several Places, viz: Lexington Kentucky, Nashville West Tennessee, Knoxville East Tennessee, Winchester, Woodstok, Staunton, Lexington, and Abington Virginia.

PREFACE.

AS the design of this Book is not to entertain the purchaser with a preface, the Author will just drop a few words explanatory to his rules and motives for ushering into the hands of the public, his present harmonical system. In this work, the Author has laid down the rudiments of music, in a form very much abridged, and as he flatters himself, has rendered them much plainer, and more easy to the understanding, than any heretofore published. From his practical knowledge as a teacher of sacred music, and his extensive acquaintance with the most eminent masters, together with the great opportunity which he has had of selecting tunes from the latest and most approved authors in that science; the publisher of this selection cherishes a fond hope, that will merit and obtain the approbation of an enlightened public, and prove of greater utility than any now in use. He is persuaded that this Book, from the superiority of the size and quality, will far excel any of the kind. In this work the purchaser will find, as in all other branches of literature, a succession of pieces suitable to the rise and progress of the learner. From this regularity of succession, a twofold advantage is derived; for, while the learner is furnished with plain and easy tunes suitable for beginners, he is also furnished with such tunes as are most commonly used in divine worship: and as the great design of this work, is to promote that useful and pleasing part of our public devotion called Psalmody; I hope that Teachers, as well as Christian Professors, will give it encouragement. As the great Author of our existance, has been pleased to favor the human family with devotional exercises so becoming and delightful, it seems reasonable they should be encouraged and supported, throughout all our divine Assemblies. In former times, and under the Jewish dispensation, those expressions of homage were directed by the Holy Spirit of God; as peculiarly becoming the *place where his honour dwelleth.*

They seem to have called on their fellow worshipers, to join in this important duty—"*O sing unto the Lord a new song—sing unto the Lord all the earth—it is a good thing to give thanks unto the Lord, and to sing praises unto thy name, O thou most high.* I have often wondered how people, who have daily opportunities of opening the sacred book, and contemplating the delightful raptures of the worshipers of old, could come into the house of God, and sit either with their mouth shut, or grining at some vain and idle speculation, while the devout worshipers are singing the praises of their Redeemer.

It was remark of an eminent writer too applicable to the present day, "The worship in which we could most resemble the inhabitants of Heaven, is the worst performed upon earth." There appears too much truth in this observation, too often does a disgraceful silence prevail in our churches, too often are dissonance and discord substituted for the charms of melody and harmony. True it is, that there are individuals among us whom Providence has not blessed with singing faculties, but will not truth oblige the most of us to confess, that the fault rests not in a want of natural abilities? but in a great carelessness and neglect of our own.

This Book is offered to the puplic in three parts, the first containing all the plain and easy tunes commonly used in our churches; secondly, a variety of the more lengthy and elegant pieces commonly used in concert, or singing societies; and lastly, the anthems. Teachers therefore would be doing justice to their employers, by teaching the pieces as here inserted.

In the following work, the Counter, or C cliff is set aside, and the g's cliff (which answers alike for tenor, treble and counter) is substituted in its stead. The counters being thus removed, and placed an octave below their former standing, and on the g's cliff, are to be sung in a treble voice when performed by a female; and in a tenor voice when performed by a man. My reason for disposing of this cliff is, that experience has proven it to be the most obscure, and difficult to understand, of any character belonging to the rudiments

"This character, or part of music called counter," says a certain scholar to his Teacher. "I do not rightly understand, from the appearance of the order in which these note stand, and agreeable to the manner in which the notes in the other parts severly occupy their staves; I, being unskilled in music, would suppose the voice to be stretch to the very pirnacle of its extent, the notes being chiefly in alt; but I find you sir, as a Teacher, sounding these notes as though they occupied but a low seat in the tenor stave, and your female voices as though they were placed quite low on the treble stave. Now, I want to know the cause of this deception; or why it is, that those notes require ledger lines in alt, and yet sounded so low?" Teacher, to answer this query, and unravel this mystery, we must refer to the scale of connection, where you will find that E 4th line in counter, exactly corresponds with E 1st line in treble, and just an octave above E 1st line in tenor; the 2 former occupying the 13th and the latter the 6th sound of the general scale; e. g let the tenor voice sound E fourth space, (which is an octave above E lower line) the counter E 4th line, and the treble E 1st line, and the sounds will be precisely the same; but the tenor sound, as above, being nearly the extent of a common voice, he is compelled, when singing counter, to strike it an octave below. in order to perform the high notes without affecting the voice, and these are the causes of those high notes having so grave a sound. "True sir, I think I understand you, but it has cost you some words, and me some perplexity; but could not all this be removed? If I mistake not you say, that the fourth line in counter, and 1st in treble are precisely the same, and I will know, that the treble and tenor are represented by the same cliff, and the only difference in the sound of the first line in treble, and the first in tenor, is, the acuteness and gravity of the Human voice; now, why not dispossess this character and substitute the gs in its stead? By this change I discover that you will be relieved from a tedious explanation, and me from an intricate study. Teacher, I find you not quite so unskilled as you pretended, and you reasoning only tends to confirm an opinion that I have been harboring for some time, and if your are agreed, I am willing to dismiss the subject without any father discussion.

THE following is a representation of the general scale, shewing the connection of the parts, and also what sound of the general scale each letter, line, or space, in either of the octaves represents. For instance, A. the natural minor key, occupies the 2nd, 9th and 16th sounds of the general scale. C. the natural major key the 4th, 11th and 18th. Thus it will appear, that every octave being unison; are considered one and the same sound. Although the last note in the Bass is always the key note, and must be either faw, or law, and in case the me is not transposed, will stand either on the 2nd, or 4th degrees as above; yet with the same propriety we may suppose them on the 9th, 11th &c. degrees: for when we refer to a pitch pipe for the sound of either of the forgoing keys, if it be properly constructed, it will exactly correspond with the 9th or 11th sound of the general scale. Then by decending the octave, we get the sound of the natural key, and by ascending a third, fourth, or fifth, as the tune may require, we may readily discover whether the piece be properly keyed. If we find, ofter decending the octave, that we can ascend to the highest note in the Tenor or Treble, so as to pronounce it with ease

GENERAL SCALE.

—◁:◈:◉:◈:▷—

			Sol
22		G space above	
21		F 5th line	Faw
20		E 4th space	Law
19		D 4th line	Sol
18		C 3rd space	Faw
17		B 3rd line —Me—	Me
16		A 2nd space	Law
15		G 2nd line	Sol
14		F 1st space	Faw
13		E 1st line	Law
		F—5th line	
12		E 4th space	Sol
11		D 4th line	Faw
10		C 3rd space	Me
9		A 5th line / B 3rd line —Me—	Law
8		G 4th space / A 2nd pace	Sol
7		F 4th line / G 2nd line	Faw
6		E 3rd space / F 1st space	Law
5		D 3rd line / E first line	Sol
4		C 2nd space the natural Major Key	Faw
3		B 2nd line —Me—	Me
2		A 1st space the natural Minor Key	Law
1		G 1st line —s—	Sol

Treble Staves. | Tenor Stave. | Bass Stave.

and freedom, the piece may be said to be rightly keyed: If on the contrary, (after decending) we find it difficult, to ascend as above, the piece is improperly key'd, and should be set lower. From this connection it aprears, that the same letter or note, that occupies the upper line of the Bass, also occupies the second space of the Tenor and Treble; and when sounded by a man or woman's voice are exactly the same: but when sounded by both, the latter being an octave more accute then the former, causes her to strike the sixteenth degree of the general scale, while he only strikes the ninth. Thus when it occurs, (as it frequently does in minor keys) that the first note of the Bass stands on the upper line, (or 9th degree of the scale,) and first note of the Tenor and Treble on the second space, they are said to be unison; and thus it is, that a man singing medius,* sounds every note as though they stood on the same line or space in Tenor, (only softer.) The same may be said of a woman singing cantus.† Although they take the same sound with the tenor, yet their voice being more accute, carries the sound an octave higher, and thereby sounds every note as if placed on the same line or space in Treble.

* Medius is low Treble, performed an octave below its proper pitch, which is always done when sung in a man's voice.

† Cantus is high Tenor, or the Tenor performed an active higher than its proper pitch, which always is done when sang by a woman

21

The foregoing scale comprises three octaves, or 22 sounds. The F Cliff when used in Bass, occupies the 7th sound of the general scale, and when in counter the 14th which is an octave higher. The G's Cliff when used in Tenor occupies the 8th, and when in Treble or counter the 15th sound of the general scale. In the followng work the counters are chiefly governed by the g's cliff, excepting a few instances in the Anthems, where the F cliff is used.

Having thus endeavoured to explain the above scale, I shall in the next place proceed to the rules for composition.

Music is naturally divided into Melody and Harmony. Melody is the agreeable effect which arises from the performance of a single part of Music only. Harmony is the pleasing union of several sounds, or the performance of the several parts of Music together. The Notes which produce Harmony when sounded together, are concords, and their intervals, are called consonant intervals. Discords, are such as when sounded together, produce a disagreeable sound to the ear. Their intervals are called disonant intervals; the concords employed together in composition, are unison, third, fifth and sixth, with their octaves. The intervals or degrees called perfect cords, are the unisons, fifths and eights. The intervals or degrees called imperfect cords, are the thirds, sharp fourths, flat fifths, and sixths. The intervals or degrees called discords, are seconds, flats fourths, sevenths, and ninths. The following Table is an example of the several concords and discords, with their octaves immediatly under them.

<table>
<tr><td>CONCORDS.</td><td>DISCORDS.</td></tr>
</table>

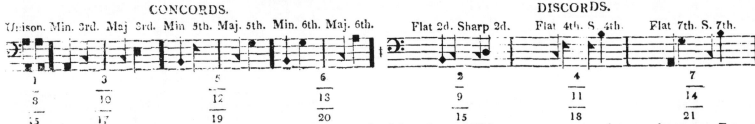

| Unison. | Min. 3rd. | Maj 3rd. | Min 5th. | Maj. 5th. | Min. 6th. | Maj. 6th. | | Flat 2d. | Sharp 2d. | | Flat 4th. | S. 4th. | | Flat 7th. | S. 7th. |

1	3		5	6		2	4	7
8	10		12	13		9	11	14
15	17		19	20		15	18	21

Notwithstanding the 2nd. 4th, and 7th, are discords. Yet, I am of opinion, that a skilful composer may use them to advantage. For, as an eminent Author observes; "They will answer a similar purpose to acid, which being tasted immediately before sweet, give the latter a more pleasing relish" as But one of the most difficult parts of composition, is, to use a discord in such place, and manner, as to show more fully the power and beauty of Music; I allow composers to use them sparingly, and always let them be immediately followed by a perfect chord. Although the 4th,, is really a discord; yet it is very frequently used in composition, and the reason is, its not being so harsh and disagreeable as the 2nd or 7th, for the harsh sound of a fourth, may be so molefied by the sweetness of the 5th and 8th, as to harmonize almost as well as any three sounds in nature. From this we may suppose, that where we have 2 perfect chords, a discord may be introduced without violating the laws, of harmony.

+ This is the bass stave, but may be applied to any other part,

RUDIMENTS OF MUSIC.

MUSICAL CHARACTERS EXPLAINED.

A Stave, - - Is five lines with their spaces on which music is written.

A Single bar Divides the time according to the measure note.

A Double bar or Shews the end of a strain.

A Close or Shews the end of a tune.

A Repeat. Shews that the tune must be again performed from the note before which it is placed, to the next double bar or close.

A Brace, Shews how many parts are performed together.

A Ledgerline is added when notes ascend or descend beyond the stave.

A Slur Shews how many notes are sung to one syllable.

The Figure 3 being placed over or under any three notes, shews that they must be performed a third quicker.

A Dot at the right hand of a note, adds to it, half its length.

The Figures 1 2 Shew that the note under 1 is sung before the repeat, and that under 2 after it; if slur'd, both are sung after it.

A Prisa ꞉||꞉ signifies that the preceding word, or sentence, must be sung to the note or notes under which it is set.

A Trill, tr or tr. signifies that the note over which it is placed should be lightly warbled, like a soft roll.

MOODS OF COMMON TIME.

1st Has a semibreve or its quantity in a measure; sung in the time of four seconds, four beats in a measure, two down, and two up.

2nd. Has the same measure note, beat in the same manner; only performed a third quicker.

3rd Has the same measure note, sung in the time of two and a half seconds, two beats in a measure, one down, and one up.

The accents in each of the foregoing moods, falls on the 1st. and 3d. parts of the bar.

4th. $\frac{2}{4}$ Has a minum for its measure note, sung in the time of one and a half seconds, two beats in a measure, one down & 1 up.

MOODS OF TRIPLE TIME

1st. is exprest 3 Has 3 minums in a measure; and 3 beats, sung in by the figures 2 the time of three seconds,, 2 beats down and 1 up.

2nd. By the $\frac{3}{4}$ figures

Has three crotchets in a measure, beat like the first, only a third faster,

3rd. By the figures 3 8⁻

Has three quavers in measure, and 2 beats, performed in the time of one and a half seconds.

COMPOUND TIME.

st. is expressed by the figures $\frac{6}{4}$

Has six quavers in a measure, sung in the time of two seconds and a half, and two beats, one down, and one up.

2nd. By the figures 6 8⁻

Has six quavers in a measure, sung in time of t second and a half, beat like the first. In these two moods the accent falls on the first & third parts of the measure.

N. B. The hand falls at the begining of every measure in all moods of time.

The F. Cliff. Represents the Bass Stave and stands on F.

The G's Cliff. Stands on G, and in this work answers alike for Tenor, Treble and Counter.

THE NATURAL PLACE FOR ME IS IN B; BUT

If B be flat - - - - - me is in - - - - - - - - - - - - E
If B E, - - - - - - - - - me is in - - - - - - - - - - - - A
If B, E, A, - - - - - me is in - - - - - - - - - - D
If B, E, A, D, - - - - me is in - - - - - - - - - - - - G

If F, be sharp - - - - me is in - - - - - - - - - - - - F
If F, C, - - - - - - - - - - me is in - - - - - - - - - - - - C
If F, C, G, - - - - - - - me is in - - - - - - - - - - - - G
If F, C, G, D, - - - - - me is in - - - - - - - - - - - - D

When me is found, the notes ascending, are, twice faw sol law, and descending, twice law sol faw, then comes me again either way.

THE PROPORTION OF THE NOTES.

1	Semibreve is equal to
2	Minims.
4	Crotchets.
8	Quavers.
16	Semiquavers.
32	Demi semi-quavers.

A Semibrive rest.
Is a Square below
the line.

A Minum rest
Is a Square a-
bove the line.

A Crotchets rest. Is
a slanted stroke with
a dash called a sutton.

A Quaver rest.
Is an inverted
sutton

A Semiquaver rest.
Is an inverted sutton
with a dash.

A Demisemiquaver
rest. Is an inverted
sutton with 2 dashes.

N B. Notes joined together at the bottom, answers the purpose of a Slur.

As soon as the learner has memorized the foregoing rules, the Teacher in order to know whether they are well understood, should interogate him in the following manner.

Question. How is the first mood of common time exprest?
Answer. By a plain C.
Q. How the 2nd?
A. By a C with a bar though it.
Q. How the 3rd?
A. By an inverted Ɔ.
Q. How the 4th?
A. By the figures two, four.
Q. How is the first mood of Treble time exprest?
A. By the figures three, two.

☞ In the 3rd line from the top in the foregoing page *read* 3 beats In the first Mood of Compound Time, for quavers *read* Crotohets.
B

Q. How the 2nd?
A. By the figures three, four.
Q. How the 3rd?
A. By the figures three, eight.
Q. How is the first mood of compound time exprest?
A. By the figures six, four.
Q. How the 2nd?
A. By the figures six, eight.
Q What do you understand by the lower figure, or figure in the first mood of Treble time?
A It shews that the semibreve which is the measure Note. is devided into 2 parts called minums
Q What by the upper figure or figure 3?
A That 3 minums or their quantity fill a measure.
Q. What do you understand by the lower figures generally?
A They serve to shew how many parts the measure Note is divided into.
Q What by the upper figures!
A They shew how many of those Divisions fill a measure.
Q. Into how many parts is the measure note divided, in the 2nd mood of Treble time?   A. Four.
Q. What are those parts called?   A. Crotchets.
Q. How many crotchets fill a measure?   A. Three.
Q. Into how many parts is the measure note divided, in the 3rd mood of Treble time?   A. Eight.
Q. What are those parts called?   A. Quavers.
Q. How many Quavers fill a measure in this mood?
A. Three.
Q. Into how many parts is the measure divided, in the first mood of compound time?   A. Four.
Q. How many of those parts fill a measure?   A. Six.

Q. Into how many parts is the measure note divided in the 2nd mood of compound time ?   A. Eight.

Q. How many of those parts fill a measure ?   A. Six

Q   What is the use of a single Bar ?

A. It divides the time according to the measure note.

Q. A double Bar ?   A. Shews the end of a strain.

Q. A Close ?   A   Shews the end of a time.

Q. A Brace ?

A. Shews how many parts are performed together.

Q. A Ledgerline ?

A   Is added when notes ascend or descend beyond the stave.

Q   The Figure 3 ?

A. Snews the notes must be performed a 3rd quicker.

Q. What are we do understand by the Figures 1, 2 at the end of a Tune ?

A. They show that the Note under 1 is sung before the repeat, & that under 2 after it ; if tied with a Slur both are sung after it.

Q   A Semibreve rest ?   A. A square below the line.

Q   A Minum rest ?   A. A spuare above the line.

Q. A Crotchet rest ?   A. A sutton.

Q. A Quaver rest ?   A. An inverted sutton.

Q. A Semiquaver rest ?

A. An inverted sutton with a dash.

Q   A Demisemiquaver rest ?

A. An inverted sutton with 2 dashes.

Q. A point set before a Note ?

A. Adds to it half its usual lenght.

Q. A Trill placed over a note ?

A. Shew that it may be softly warbled.   ☞ See Example, Page 12.

Q. How is the Key Note known ?

A. By the last note of the Bass, which is always the next above or below Me, if above, it is a Sharp Key, if below it is a Flat Key.

A half note may serve to represent the semitones between me and faw, and law and faw.

The treangle is faw, the round is sol the square law, and the deamond me.

Faw   Sol   Law   Me

GENERAL OBSERVATIONS.

A proper accent is a very essential ornament in singing, and should be carefully attended to, for if the poetry is good, and the music well adapted, accented syllable will always fall on the accented parts of the measure. For instance : if the poetry begins with a trochee, the hand should fall on the first note, if with an Iambus it should raise. Some authors are opposed to two accents when the measure is divided into two parts, but in this case, I would ask what is to be done with a spondee, where both the words or syllables are accented : but to be short, I would just observe, that when it so happens, that accented words falls on the unaccented part of the measure, language must predominate.

A genteel pronounciation is another excellence that should be inculcated ; many who are otherwise excellent Singer, obscure the ideas the tuter in melody, by pronouncing ungramatically. Words terminating in ly, ny, &c. are apt to be pronounced as though they formed a seperate word, which not only destroys the beauty of the Music, but sense of the poetry ; The best rule therefore that can be given is, to pronounce according to the proper mode of speaking, so that what we sing may also be understood.

Youngsters should not be forgetful of the importance of the calling in which they are engaged, but remember that a becoming seriousness should at all time prevail when using sacred words, our thoughts ought always to correspond with the music and subject, and by these means we would find ourselves delighted with that solemnity, that should accompany the sacred worship of the Deity.

Young singers should be very industrious in acquiring a graceful manner of beating time, and should be careful not to contract any disagreeable habits, as they are hard to overcome.

All distortion of the limbs or features while singing, has a tendency to excite ridicule, and should be carefully avoided. Nothing is more disgusting in singers, than affected quirks and ostentatious parade, endeavouring to overpower other voices by the strength of their own, or officiously assisting other parts while theirs is silent. On the other hand, nothing is more praise worthy in a choir of singers, than a becoming deportment, and a solemnity which should accompany an exercise so near a kin to that, which will through all eternity engage the attention of those who walk in "climes of bliss."

There should be no noise in time of singing, except the music alone, all whispering, laughing, talking, or struting about the floor, is ridiculous in time of school, and should not be suffered.

Young singers, should not join in concert, until each can sing their own part correctly. Too long singing at one time injures the lungs. A cold or cough, all kinds of spiritous liquors, long fasting, &c. &c. are destructive to the voice of one who is much in the practice of singing : A frequent use of spiritous liquors will speedily ruin the best voice.

Flat keyed tunes, should be sung softer than sharp keyed ones, and may be proportioned with a lighter bass, but for sharp keyed tunes let the bass be full and strong, but not harsh.

The proper proportion of the parts is generally said, to be 3 on the bass, 1 on the the tenor, 1 on the counter, and 2 on the treble ; but I think two on bass sufficient for the other proportions, particularly in flat keyed tunes.

Teachers of Music should be particular to inculcate soft singing, for a person who practises soft singing, will retain the power of hearing, and conforming to other voices, and may readily become master of such gestures and expressions as reason and propriety dictates : Soft singing is in fact the best expedient for refining the ear and improving the voice ; "A good voice" says Mr Lewis, "may soon be much injured by too loud singing".

Let the bass be sung full and bold, the tenor regular and distinct, the counter clear and plain, the treble soft and delicate.

"Teachers" says Little and Smith, ' commit an imperceptable error in singing to much their pupils, and allowing them to unite in concert before they can perform their parts seperately ; " The best way therefore to improve scholars is, to exercise the parts seperately till they are capable of performing truly by themselves ; The teacher should occationally sing the part by himself, then after going over several times with the scholars ; let them try it by themselves, and continue on in this way, frequently repeating the places where he discovers the greatest deficiency.

All solos should be sung softer than the parts when moving together.

Teachers should sing but few tunes at a time, and continue at them till they are well understood ; to skim over 40 or 50 tunes of an evening is no way to improve scholars, it gives them a habit of raking through their books, and wishing to know something about every tune, before they understand one piece properly.

The high notes, quick notes, and slurred notes of each part, should be sung softer than the low, long, and single notes of the same part.

27

As the performing of the several moods in their proper time, is a matter of great importance; I have thought advisable to give rules for the construction of a pendulum that will vibrate once for every beat in the several moods here laid down. Take a round wooden ball, the size whereof is immaterial about an inch in diameter is perhaps as suitable as any; suspend it by a silken cord, in such a manner as to swing each way without interruption; let the length of the cord, from the ball to the pin from which it is suspended, be as follows:

For the plain C, C with a bar thro' it, 3 2, & 3 4. 39 & 2 10ths inches
For the ↄ inverted, and 6 4 - - - - - - 61 & 25 100th do
For 2 4, 3 8, and 6 8, - - - - - - - 22   do
Then for every swing or vibration of the ball. count one beat.

The motion and resting of the hand, may be considered as dividing the beats equally in common and treble time, in compound time the resting is double of the motion.

Examples of Common Time

Treble Time

Compound Time

The figures in the above examples shew the number of beats to a measure, the letters *d* and *u* shew the beat to be down or up, and the letters *m* and *r* the motion and resting of each beat.

Let the accent always be governed by the motion of the hand, the strongest when the hand is falling, and when there is two accents in a measure, the weakest when rising

The Eight Notes

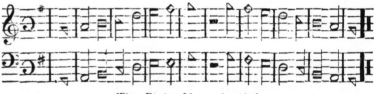

The Eight Notes doubled

A Syncope   A Syncopation   Examples of the trill

ROCKBRIDGE. L. M. Sharp Key on C. 9

Sweet is the work, my God, my King, To shew thy love by morning light, and talk of all thy truths at night.
To praise thy name, give thanks and sing;

LENOX. P. M. Sharp Key on C.

Blow ye the trumpet blow, Let all the nations know, The year of Jubilee is come, Return ye ransom'd sinners home.
The gladly solemn sound; To earth's remotest bound.

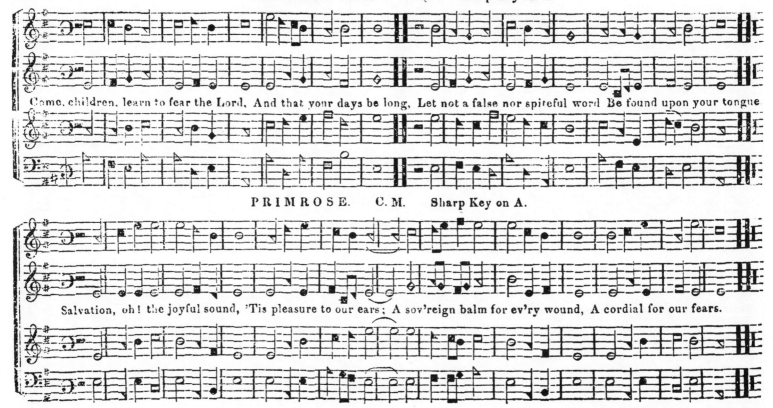

ROCHESTER. C. M. Sharp Key on A.

Come, children, learn to fear the Lord, And that your days be long, Let not a false nor spiteful word Be found upon your tongue.

PRIMROSE. C. M. Sharp Key on A.

Salvation, oh! the joyful sound, 'Tis pleasure to our ears; A sov'reign balm for ev'ry wound, A cordial for our fears.

ALBION. C. M. Sharp Key on G.

And must this body die, This mortal frame decay ; And must these active limbs of mine Lie mould'ring in the clay.

WELLS. L. M. Sharp Key on G.

Ye nations round the earth rejoice, Before the Lord your sov'reign King, Serve him with cheerful heart and voice. With all your

tongues his glory sing

WALSAL. C. M. Flat Key on A.

SUPPLICATION L. M. Flat Key on A.

AYLESBURY. S M. Flat Key on A.

The Lord my Shepherd is. I shall be well supply'd, Since he is mine and I am his, What can I want beside

WINDHAM. L M. Flat Key on F.

Broad is the road that leads to death, And thousands walk together there: Broad is the road that leads to death, With here and there a traveler.

KEDRON.   L M.   Flat Key on E.

How pleasant, how divinely fair,
O Lord of hosts, thy dwellings are!   With long desire my spirit faints,   To rise & dwell among thy saints.

GEORGIA.   C. M.   Flat Key on E.

Return, O God of love, return, Earth is a tiresome place;   How long shall we thy children mourn   Our absence from thy face.

Come humble sinner in whose breast A thousand thoughts revolve; I'll go to Jesus, tho' my sins Hath like a mountain rose;
Come with your guilt and fear oppress'd. And make this last resolve. I know his courts, I'll enter in. Whatever may oppose

DUBLIN. C. M. Flat Key on A.

Lord what is man, poor feeble man, Born of the earth at first, His life a shadow, light and vain, Still hast'ning to the dust.

NEW-ORLEANS C. M. Flat Key on E.

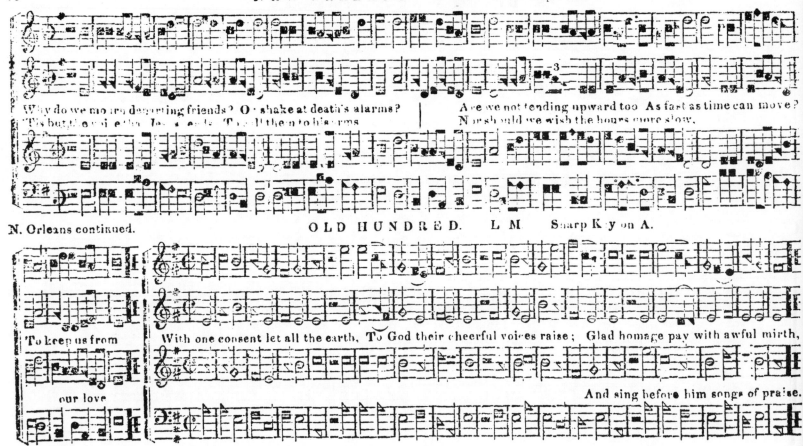

Why do we mourn departing friends? O shake at death's alarms?
'Tis but the voice that Jesus sends, To call them to his arms.

Are we not tending upward too As fast as time can move?
Nor should we wish the hours more slow.

N. Orleans continued.

To keep us from

our love

OLD HUNDRED. L M Sharp Key on A.

With one consent let all the earth, To God their cheerful voices raise; Glad homage pay with awful mirth,

And sing before him songs of praise.

TENDER THOUGHT.   L. M.   Flat Key on A.

Arise, my tender thoughts, arise,
To torrents melt my streaming eyes;

And thou, my heart, with anguish feel,
Those evils which thou canst not heal.

ST. MARTINS.   C. M.   Sharp Key on A.

With cheerful notes let all the earth, To heav'n their voices raise. Let all inspir'd with Godly mirth, Sing solemn hymns of praise.

MEAR. C. M. Sharp Key on G.

In God's own house pronounce his praise, His grace he there reveals; To heaven your joy and wonder raise, For there his glory dwells.

LIBERTY HALL. C. M. Flat Key on A.

Death! what a solemn word to all! What mortal things are men! We just arise and soon we fall, To mix with earth again.

LITTLE MARLBOROUGH. S. M. Flat Key on A.

Lord, what a feeble piece Is this our mortal frame! Our life! how poor a trifle 'tis, That scarce deserves the name!

NINETY-THIRD. S. M. Sharp Key on C.

My Saviour and my King, Thy beauties are divine ; Thy lips with blessings overflow, And every grace is thine.

CHINA. C. M. Sharp Key on D.

Why should we mourn departing friends, Or shake at death's alarms, 'Tis but the voice that Jesus sends, To call them to his arms.

CONSOLATION. C. M. Flat Key on A.

Once more, my soul, the rising day salutes thy waking eyes; Once more, my voice, my tribute pay, To him that rules the sky.

I lift my soul to God ; My trust is in his name ; Let not my foes that seek my blood, Still triumph in my shame, Still triumph, &c.

ST. THOMAS.   S. M.   Sharp Key on A.

Hark, it is wisdom's voice, That spreads itself around Come hither all ye sons of death, And listen to the sound.

HIDING PLACE. L. M. Flat Key on G

Hail sov'reign love that first began The scheme to rescue fallen man; Hail matchless, free, eternal grace, That gave my soul a hiding place.

SUFFIELD. C. M. Flat Key on E.

Teach me the measure of my days, Thou Maker of my frame, I would survey life's narrow space, And learn how frail I am.

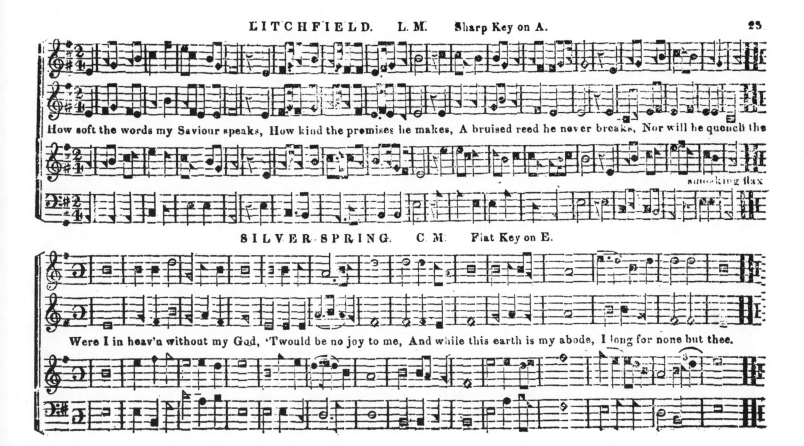

LITCHFIELD. L. M. Sharp Key on A.

How soft the words my Saviour speaks, How kind the promises he makes, A bruised reed he never breaks, Nor will he quench the smoking flax

SILVER SPRING. C. M. Flat Key on E.

Were I in heav'n without my God, 'Twould be no joy to me, And while this earth is my abode, I long for none but thee.

JUDGEMENT. L M. Flat Key on A.

My God, what inward grief I feel, When impious men transgress thy will! | Does not my soul detest & hate The sons of malice & deceit
I mourn to hear their lips profane, Take thy tremendous name in vain. | Those that oppose thy laws, and thee, I count for en-

Continued

FUNERAL THOUGHT. C. M. Flat Key on A.

emies to me Death! 'tis a melancholy day To those that have no God. When the poor soul is forc'd away To seek her last abode.

Behold the man three score and ten, Upon a dying bed, Has run his race and got no grace, An awful sight indeed   Poor man he lies

in sore surprize, And thus he doth complain, No grace

Continued.   IDUMEA.   S. M.   Flat Key on A.

I've got, and I cannot, Recall   My God, my life, my love, To thee, to thee I call: I cannot live if thou remove, For thou art all in all.

my time again.

BRANFORD. C. M. Flat Key on E.

Save me, O God, the swelling floods Break in upon my soul: I sink; and sorrow o'er my head Like mighty waters roll.

UNION. C. M. Sharp Key on C.

Lo, what an entertaining sight Are brethren that agree; Brethren, whose cheerful hearts unite In bands of piety.

NEW-JERSEY. L. M. Flat Key on A.

Behold the Lord ascending high, No more to bleed no more to die. He died, the heav'ns in mourning stood; He rises and appears to God.

BETHEL. C. M. Sharp Key on C.

Let Zion and her sons rejoice ; Behold the promis'd hour ; Her God hath heard her mourning voice, And comes t' exalt her pow'r

MILINDA. L M. Flat Key on E.

In vain the wealthy mortals toil, & heap their shining dust in vain; | Their golden cordials cannot ease Their pained hearts or aching
Look down, & scorn the humble poor, & boast their lofty hills of gain | heads; Nor fright, nor bribe, approaching death from glittering

Continued.   ZION's HILL   S. M.   Sharp Key on F.

roofs & downy beds   How beauteous are their feet, Who stand on Zion's hill! Who bring salvation on their tongues. And words of

peace reveal !

BRAY. C. M. Sharp Key on G.

29

Awake my heart, arise my tongue, Prepare a tuneful voice, In God the life of all my joys, Aloud will I rejoice   Aloud, &c.

VIRGINIA. C. M. Flat Key on E.

Thy words the raging winds controul, And rule the boist'rous deep, Thou mak'st the sleeping billows roll The rolling billows sleep.

ENFIELD.   C. M.   Sharp Key on D.

Before the rosy dawn of day, To thee my God I'll sing ; Awake my soft and tuneful lyre, Awake each charming string. Awake and

let thy flowing strains, Glide thro' the midninght air, While high

Continued.

amidst her silent orb, The

silver moon rolls clear.

LEBANON.   C. M.   Flat Key on A.

Oh glorious type of heavenly grace ! Thus Christ the Lord appears! While sinners curse, the Saviour

prays, and pities them with tears.

30

50

FIDUCIA.   C. M.   Minor Key on A.

Father, I long, I faint to see, The place of thine abode ;
I'd leave thine earthly court, and flee, Up to thy seat, my God!

Here I behold thy distant face, And 'tis a pleasing sight,
But to abide in thine embrace, Is infinite delight.

NEWBURY.   C. M.   Flat Key on A.

Lord, in the morning thou shalt hear My voice ascending high ; To thee will I direct my pray'r, To thee lift up mine eye.

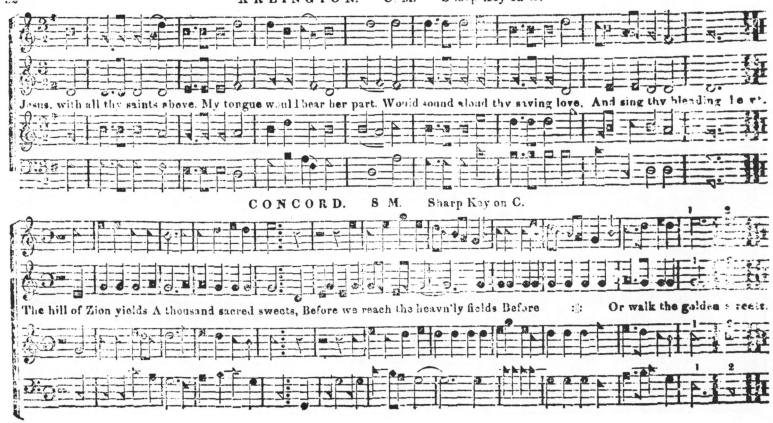

ARLINGTON. C. M. Sharp Key on G.

Jesus, with all thy saints above, My tongue would bear her part, Would sound aloud thy saving love, And sing thy bleeding heart.

CONCORD. S. M. Sharp Key on C.

The hill of Zion yields A thousand sacred sweets, Before we reach the heavn'ly fields Before :‖: Or walk the golden streets.

God of my life look gently down, Behold the pains I feel,   But I am dumb before thy throne,   Nor dare dispute thy   will.

E   FLANDRRS I. M. Sharp Key on E.

The saints shall flourish in his days, Drest in the robes of joy and praise ; Peace, like a river from his throne, Shall flow to nations yet unknown

TRIBULATION. C. M. Flat Key on D.

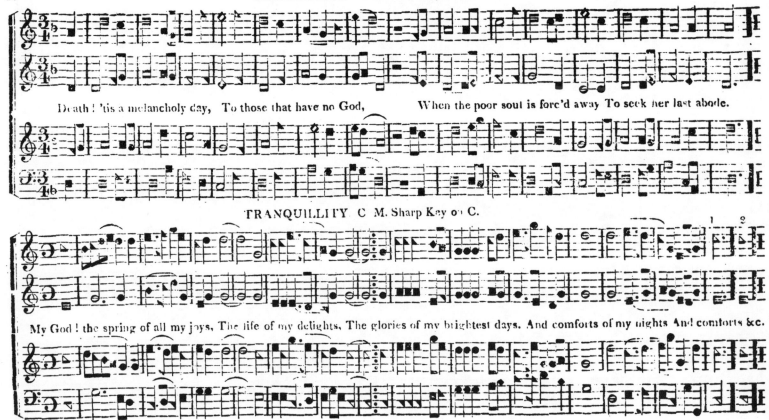

Death! 'tis a melancholy day,   To those that have no God,   When the poor soul is forc'd away To seek her last abode.

TRANQUILLITY. C. M. Sharp Key on C.

My God! the spring of all my joys, The life of my delights, The glories of my brightest days. And comforts of my nights And comforts &c.

AMANDA. L. M. Flat Key on A.

Death like an over - flowing stream, Sweeps us away; our life's a dream, An empty tale a morning flower Cut down and wither'd in an hour.

GLASGOW   L. M. Sharp Key on G.

This life's a dream, an empty show, But the bright world to which I go, Hath joys substantial and sincere, When shall I wake & find me there.

O glorious hour ! O blest abode ? I shall be near, and like my God ; And flesh and sin no more control The sacred pleasures of my soul.

35

PART II.

CONTAINING

THE MORE LENGTHY AND ELEGANT PIECES, COMMONLY USED IN CONCERT,

OR

SINGING SOCIETIES.

SOPHRONIA. P. M. or 10 & 8 Flat Key on D.

Forbear, my friends forbear, And ask no more Where all my cheerful joys are fled? Why will you make me talk my torments o'er? my life, my joy. my comfort's dead.

And must this body die, This mortal frame decay? Lie mould'ring in the clay! And must &c.

And must these active limbs of mine. And must &c. And

Continued. NEW - MONMOUTH· 8 & 7 Flat Key on A.

in the clay Lie &c.

Streams of mercy never ceasing,

mo- uld'ring in &c. Come thou fount of ev'ry blessing, Tune my heart to sing thy grace; Calls for songs of loudest praise

Come sound his praise abroad, And hymns of glory sing; Jehovah is the sov'reign God, The universal King. Jehovah is &c.

LAMBERTON. S M. Flat key on A,

this the kind return, And these the thanks we owe? Thus to abuse eternal love, Whence all our blessings flow? Thus to abuse &c.

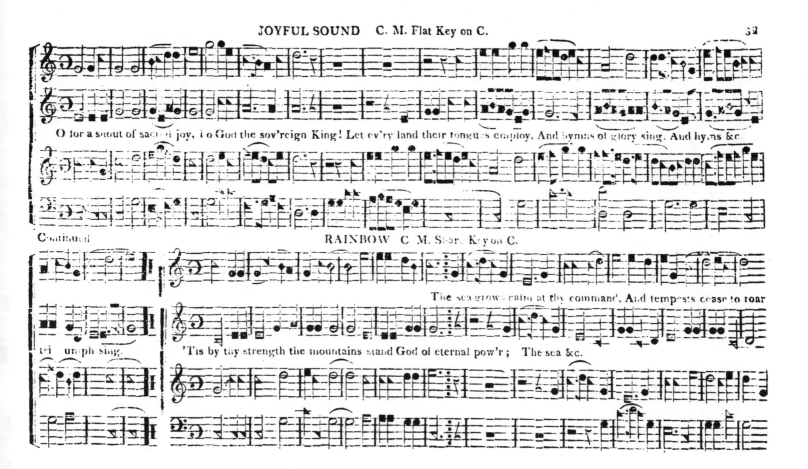

O for a shout of sacred joy, to God the sov'reign King! Let ev'ry land their tongues employ, And hymns of glory sing. And hymns &c.

Continued

RAINBOW   C. M. Sharp Key on C.

The sea grows calm at thy command, And tempests cease to roar

triumph sing.

'Tis by thy strength the mountains stand God of eternal pow'r;   The sea &c.

RAINBOW Continued.

And tempests &c.

VERGENNES C. M. Flat Key on G.

While far from home abode; and

My heart & flesh cry out for thee, When shall I tread thy courts

The sparrow builds herself a nest, And suffers no remove;

see My Saviour and my God.

O make me like the sparrow blest, To dwell but where I love. O make &c.

God is our refuge in distress, A present help when dangers press. In him undaunted we'll confide, 'Tho' earth were from her centre

tost, And mountains in the ocean lost, Torn piecemeal by the roaring tide.

Continued. AMERICA. S.M. Flat Key on A.

Torn piecemeal, &c. My soul repeat his praise, Whose mercies are so great; Whose anger is so slow to rise, So ready to abate

MONTGOMERY.　C M.　Sharp Key on C.

Early my God without delay,　I haste to seek thy face,　My thirsty spirit faints away,　Without thy cheering grace.

So pilgrims on the scorching sand, Beneath the burning sky; Long for a cooling stream at hand, and they must drink or die.

Great God attend while Sion Sings, The joy that from thy presence springs ; To spend one day with thee on earth, Exceeds a thou-

sand days of mirth.　　　　To spend, &c.

REPENTANCE. C. M. Flat Key on E.

Oh, if my soul was form'd for woe, How would I vent my sighs; Repentance would like rivers flow from both my streaming eyes 'Twas

for my sins my dearest Lord, Hung on the cursed tree, And groan'd away his dying life, For thee, my soul, for thee, for thee, &c.

FLORIDA. S. M. Flat Key on E.

Let sinners take their course, And choose the road to death ; But in the worship of my God, I'll spend my daily breath   But in &c.

GARDEN. L. M. Flat Key on A.

The grove, &c.   The grove, &c.

God, from his cloudy cistern, pours
On the parch'd earth enriching show'rs :

The grove, the garden, and the field, A thousand joyful blessings yield.

NEW-DURHAM.   C. M.   Flat Key on D.

Hark from the tombs, a doleful sound, Mine ears attend the cry ! Ye living men come view the ground, Where you must shortly lie.

Continued.

NINETY-FIFTH.   C. M.   Sharp Key on G.

Ye living, &c.   When I can read my title clear, To mansions in the skies I bid farewell to eve'ry fear, to eve'ry fear, And wipe my

I bid   I bid

weeping eyes.

I send the joys of earth away ye tempters of the mind, False as the smooth deceitful sea, And empty as the whistling wind. Your

streams were floating me along Down to the gulph of black despair, And while I listen'd to your song, Your streams had o'en convey'd

me there.

WHITESTOWN. L. M. Flat Key on E.

Remember, Lord, our mortal state,
How frail! our lives! how short the date!

Where is the man that draws his breath, Safe from disease, secure from death?

Lord, while we see whole

nations die, Our flesh and sense repine and cry, Must death forever rage and reign? Or hast thou made mankind in vain?

Oh, if my soul was form'd for woe, How would I vent my sighs; Repentance would like rivers flow from both my streaming eyes

G

'Twas for my sins my

Hung on the cursed tree. And groan'd away his dying life, For thee, my soul, for thee, for thee, &c.

dearest Lord,

HUNTINGTON. L. M. Sharp Key on A.

Lord, what a tho'tless wretch was I, To mourn & murmur & repine, To see the wicked plac'd on high, In pride & robes of honor shine

But O their end their dread.

On slipp'ry rocks I see them stand And fiery billows roll below.

ful end, Thy sanctuary taught me s - - - - - e.

Lord what a thoughtless wretch was I, To mourn & murmur & repine; To see the wicked plac'd on high, In pride & robes of honor shine.

But, Oh their end, their dreadful end ! Thy sanctuary taught me so, On slip'ry rocks I see them stand, And fiery billows roll below.

OCEAN. C. M. Sharp Key on F.

Thy works of glory mighty Lord, That rule the boist'rous sea, The sons of courage shall record, Who tempt the dangerous way.

At thy command the winds arise, And swell the towering waves, The men astonished mount the skies, And sink in gaping graves.

DELIGHT. P M Flat Key on E

No burning heats by day, Nor blasts of evening air, Shall take my health away, If God be with me there.

Thou art my sun, And thou my shade, To

guard my head, by night or noon. Thou, &c.

MOUNT SION. S M. Sharp Key on A.

The hill of Sion yields, A thousand sacred sweets; Before we reach the heav'nly fields, Or walk the golden streets,

Then let your songs abound,

Let every tear be dry, We're marching thro' Emanuel's ground, To fairer worlds on high. We're marching thro', :||: :||: We're

To

march- ing through

fairer worlds, To fairer worlds, To fairer worlds on high. We're marching, &c.

march- ing through Emanuel's ground,

WILLIAMSTOWN. L. M. Flat Key on G.

Shew pity Lord, O Lord forgive, Let a repenting sinner live; Are not thy mercies large and free? May not a sinner trust in thee?

BALLOON L.M. Flat Key on E.

Behold I fall before thy face. My only refuge is thy grace, No outward form can make me clean. The leprosy lies deep within. No bleeding

bird nor bleeding beast, Nor hyssop branch, nor sprinkling priest; Nor running brook, nor flood nor sea, Can wash the dismal stain away

Hail the day that saw him rise, Ravish'd from our wishful eyes; Christ awhile to mortals giv'n Reascends his native heav'n.

H

There the pompous triumph waits, Lift your heads eternal gates, Wide unfold the radient scene, Take the king of glory in.

SYMPHONY. P. M. Sharp Key on E.

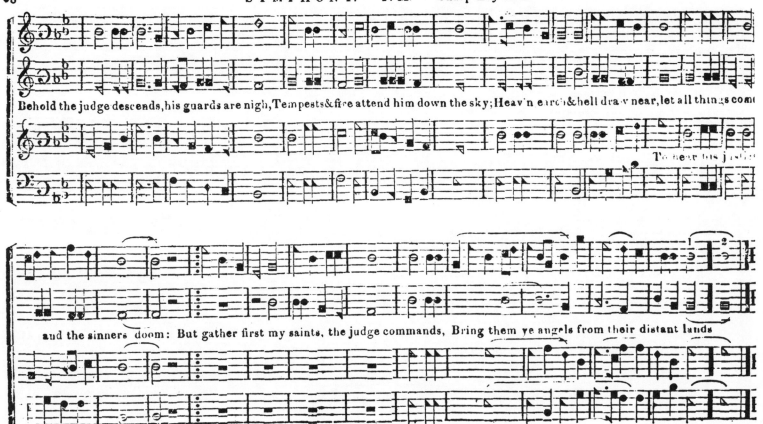

Behold the judge descends, his guards are nigh, Tempests & fire attend him down the sky; Heav'n earth & hell draw near, let all things come

To hear his justice

and the sinners' doom: But gather first my saints, the judge commands, Bring them ye angels from their distant lands

Thro' ev'ry age eternal God, Thou art our rest our safe abode, High was thy throne ere heav'n was made, High was, &c.

Or earth thy humble footstool laid.   Or earth, &c.   Or earth, &c.

SCHENECTADY. L. M. Shark key-on E.

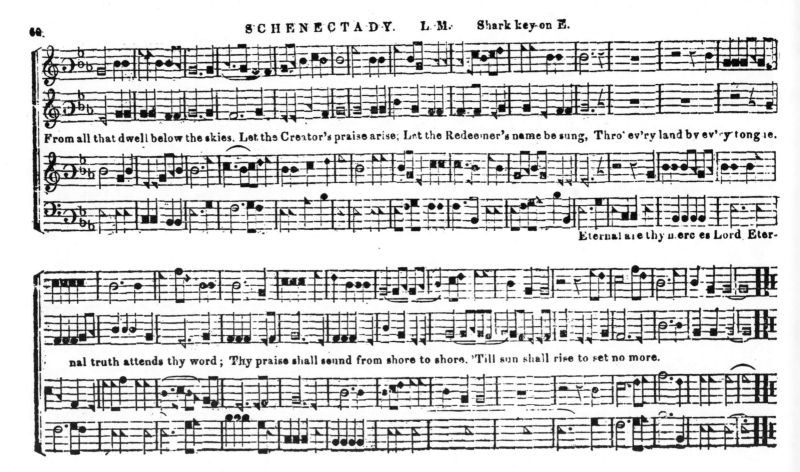

From all that dwell below the skies, Let the Creator's praise arise; Let the Redeemer's name be sung, Thro' ev'ry land by ev'ry tongue.

Eternal are thy mercies Lord, Eter-

nal truth attends thy word; Thy praise shall sound from shore to shore, 'Till sun shall rise to set no more.

If angels sung a Saviour's birth. If angels sung a Saviour's birth On that auspicious morn

If angels sung a Saviour's, Saviour's birth. On that auspicious morn.

If angels sung a Saviour's birth, If angels sung a Saviour's. Saviour's birth, on that auspicious morn,   We

If angels sung a Saviour's birth, If angels sung a Saviour's birth, On that auspicious morn, We well may imi-

We well   Now   Now   Now

We well may imi - tate their mirth, Now he again is born   Now he again. Now he again is born.

well may imitate their mirth. We well, &c.   Now, &c.   Now he again is born.

tate their mirth. We, &c.   Now he again is born, Now, &c.

NEW JERUSALEM. C M. Sharp Key on G.

The

From the third heav'n where God resides That holy happy place, The New Jerusalem comes down, Adorn'd with shining grace.

The

The, &c.

A- dorn'd with shining grace.

How did his flowing tears condole, As a for brother dead. And fasting, mortify'd his soul, While for their lives he pray'd.

They groan'd & curs'd him on their beds, Yet still he pleads & mourns, And double blessings on his head, The righteous Lord returns.

BRIDGEWATER. L M. Sharp Key on C.

Sweet is the work my God my King, To praise thy name give thanks & sing. To shew the love by morning light, And talk of all thy truths

at night.

RUSSIA. L.M. Flat Key on A.

False are the men of high degree, The baser sort are vanity ; Laid in a balance both appear Light as a puff of empty air.

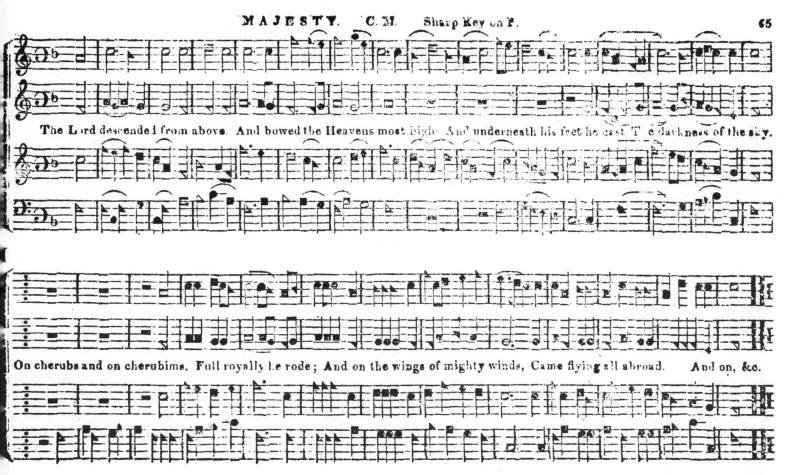

The Lord descended from above. And bowed the Heavens most high. And underneath his feet he cast The darkness of the sky.

On cherubs and on cherubims. Full royally he rode; And on the wings of mighty winds, Came flying all abroad. And on, &c.

BRISTOL. L. M. Sharp Key on F.

The lofty pillars of the sky. And spacious concave rais'd on high. Spangled with stars, a shining frame, Their great original proclaim

The unweari'd sun from day to day, Pours knowledge on his golden ray! And publishes to ev'ry land The works of an Almighty hand.

Thy wrath lies heavy on my soul. And waves of sorrow o er me roll, While dust & silence spread the gloom:

My friends belov'd in happier days, The

dear companions of my ways, Descend around me to the tomb. My friends, &c.

GRAFTON. C. M. Sharp Key on C.

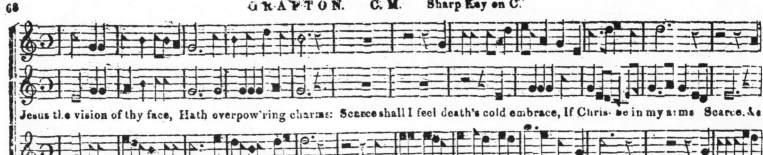

Jesus the vision of thy face, Hath overpow'ring charms: Scarce shall I feel death's cold embrace, If Christ be in my arms Scarce. &c

If Christ &c   If Christ, &c   Then while you hear my heart strings break, How sweet the minutes roll

NORWICH. S. M. Flat Key on A.

SHERBURNE. C M. Sharp Key on D.

While shepherds watch'd their flocks by night, All seated on the ground, The angel of the Lord came down and glory shone around.

Continued.

The angel &c.

MORTALITY. C M. Flat Key on E.

Stoop down my tho'ts that used to rise,
Converse awhile with death;

Think how a gasping mortal lies, And pants

away his b e th

Think how a gasping &c.

WESLEY. C M Flat Key on A.

Dear Sov'reign &c. And bring. And bring the promis'd day An &c.

With inward pain my heart strings sound My soul dissolves away. Dear Sov'reign whirl the seasons round, And bring. And bring &c. :|||:

Dear Sov'reign whirl the seasons round, Dear &c. And bring. :|||: :|||: the promis'd day

Dear Sov'reign whirl the seasons round, Dear &c And bring, :|: the promis'd day, And &c

*BERNE   C. M.   Flat Key on A.

hear me O Lord, nor hide thy face, But answer least I die ; Hast thou not built a throne of grace, To hear when sinners cry.   My

days are wasted like the smoke,   dissolving in the air,   My strength is dry'd my heart is broke,   And sinking in despair.

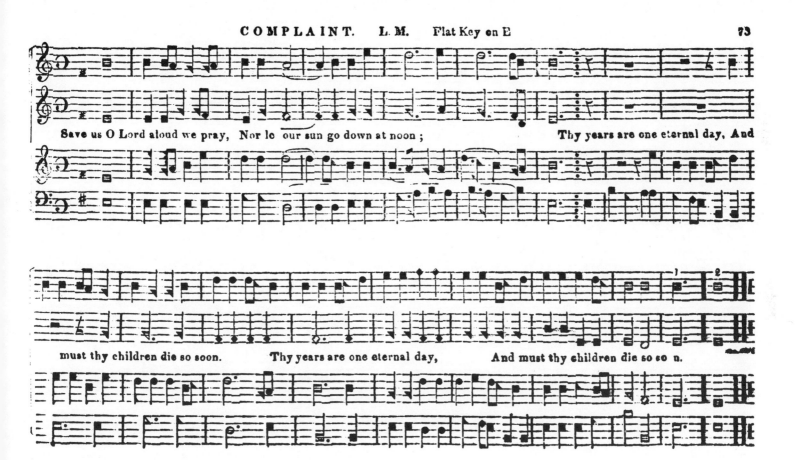

Save us O Lord aloud we pray, Nor le our sun go down at noon ; Thy years are one eternal day, And

must thy children die so soon. Thy years are one eternal day, And must thy children die so so n.

ALL·SAINTS·NEW. L.M. Flat Key on D.

Oh! if my Lord would come & meet My soul would stretch her wings in haste; For fearless thro' death's iron gate, Nor fee the terror as

she pass'd

Jesus can make a dying bed Feel soft as downy pillows are. While on his breast I lean While on his breast I lean.

Jesus &c

While

Jesus can make a dying &c.

While

And breathe

Jesus can &c.

While on his breast I lean my head, And breathe my life out sweetly there

I lean my head and breathe my &c.   and breathe,   my life out sweetly there

out sweetly there And breathe my life out sweetly there.   And breathe,   my life out sweely there

While on his breast I lean, I lean   my head, And breathe,   my life out sweetly there.

SUTTON   C M   Flat Key on F.

Save me, O God, the swelling floods, Break in upon my soul ; I sink, & sorrows o'er my head, Like mighty waters roll Like &c.

PENNSYLVANIA   L M   Flat Key on G

When shall thy lovely face be seen?
When shall our eyes behold our God?

What length of distance lies between,
And hills of guilt? a heavy load!

Our months are a &c

Fly, winged time. &c.

of cla, and slow ve ry moment wears:

Fly, winged time &c

Fly, winged time. &c

Fly, winged time, and roll away, These tedious rounds of sluggish years. Fly, &c.   and re-

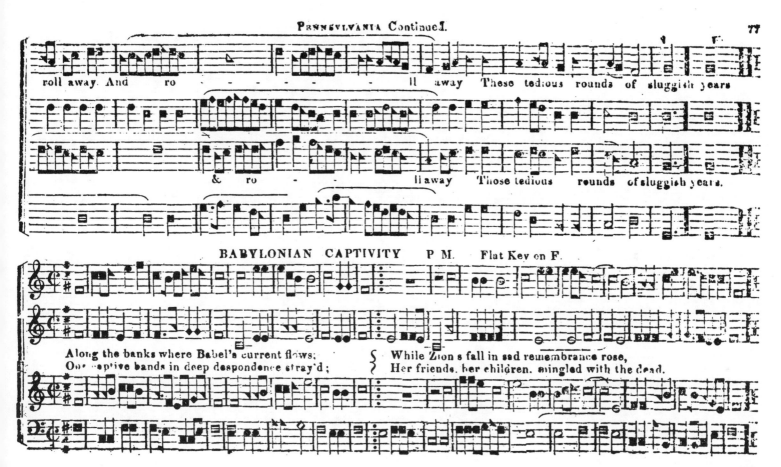

roll away. And   ro - - - - ll away These tedious rounds of sluggish years

& ro - - ll away Those tedious rounds of sluggish years.

BABYLONIAN CAPTIVITY   P. M.   Flat Key on F.

Along the banks where Babel's current flows;
One captive bands in deep despondence stray'd;

While Zion's fall in sad remembrance rose,
Her friends, her children, mingled with the dead.

JERUSALEM. L M. Sharp Key on D.

This line's a dream, an empty show, But the bright world to which I go Hath joys substanial & incere W e shal awake, ::: and be

there   O glorious hour. O blest abode, I shall be near, And like my God, :‖: And flesh & sin no more control The sacred pleasures,

of the soul. My flesh shall slumber in the ground, Till the last trumpet's joyful sound; Then burst the

Continued

DOVER. L M Sharp Key on C

chains with sweet surprise And in my Saviour's image rise, And in &c

My soul thy great creater praise; When cloth'd in his

celestial rays He in full

majesty appears.
And like a robe his glory wears.

The heav'ns are for his curtains spread;
Th' unfathom'd deep he makes his bed;

Clouds are his chariot when he flies
On winged storms across the skies.

A M I T Y.   P M   Sharp Key on A

How pleas'd & bless'd was I.
To hear the people cry,

Come let us seek our God to day;

Yes with a cheerful zeal,
We haste to Zion's hill.

And there our vows and honors pay

Thou great & sovereign Lord of all,
Whom heav'nly hosts obey: Around whose throne dread thunders roll, and livid lightnings play   Around whose &c

pla   y   &lvid lightning play   Around whose &c

Play   Pla - y   Around &c

livid lightnings play. &livid lightnings play   Around &c

CALVARY. C. M. Flat Key on A.

My thoughts &c.

My tho'ts that often mount the skies, Go

Where,&c.   And ow - ns.   her &

search the world beneath. Where nature all in ruin lies, where, &c. And ow - ns,   her sov'reign death.

EXHORTATION.   L M   Flat Key on A.

Now in the heat of youthful blood. Remember your creator God; Behold the months come hast'ning on, When you shall say my

joys are gone.   When you &c

From low pursuits exalt my mind
From ev'ry vice of ev'ry kind
Nor let my conduct ever tend, To wound the

feelings of a friend.

Though golden flow'rs my path should trace,
And joys salute me as I pass,

Yet may my gen'rous bosom know,
And learn to feel another's woe

CREATION S M Sharp Key ou A

Let ev'ry creature join To praise th' eternal God; Ye heav'ly host, the song begin, And sound his name abroad. Thou sun with golden

...rays, And moon with paler rays, And moon &c. Ye starry lights, ye twinkling flames. Shine to your Maker's praise. Shine &c.

How did my heart rejoice to hear My friends devoutly say,
In Zion let us all appear, And keep the solemn day!

And keep the &c.

I love her gates, I love the road;
The Church adorn'd with grace,

Stands like a palace built for God.
To shew his milder face

Stands like &c   Up to her courts, with joys unknown, The holy tribes repair; The Son of David

NEWBURGH. S M. Sharp Key on C.

holds his throne. And sits in

judgment there

Let ev'ry creature join, To praise th' eternal God ; Ye heavenly host the songs begin, And

sound his name abroad

{ Thou sun with golden beams,   { Ye starry lights, ye twinkling flames, }
{ And moon with paler rays;   { Shine to your maker s praise.   } Ye starry &c

I'll praise my Maker with my breath;
And when my voice is lost in death,
Praise shall employ my nobler pow'rs;
My days of praise shall ne'er be past,
While life, and thought, and being, last,

Or immortality endures My days of praise shall ne'r be past &c.

STAFFORD S M Sharp Key on A

See what a living stone. The builders did refuse, Yet God hath built his Church thereon, Yet God, &c In spite of env'ous Jews

IMMENSITY S M Flat Key on A

Within thy circling pow'r I stand. On ev'ry side I find thy hand ; Awake, asleep, at home. abroad, I am surrounded still with God.

Young people all attention give,   I want your souls in Christ to live,   Remember you are hast'ning on
And hear what I do say;   In everlasting day   To death's dark gloomy shade

M

Remember you, &c   Your joys on earth will soon be gone,   Your flesh in dust be laid

DOMINION. L.M. Sharp Key on E

Jesus shall reign where er the sun
Does his successive journies run:

His kingdom stretch from shore to shore
"Till moons shall wax and wane no more.

His &c.

DOMINION CONTINUED

His &c. His &c.

His Kingdom &c.

CARLISLE L.M. Flat Key on A.

Deep in our hearts let us record, The deeper sorrows of our Lord

Behold the rising billows ro - ll, To overwhelm his holy so - ul. To overwhelm &c.

WORTHINGTON CM Flat Key on D.

Thee we adore eternal name And humbly own to thee, How feeble is our mortal frame. How, &c. What dying worms are we. What, &c.

Fly like a tim'rous trembling dove. Fly like &c.   To distant mounta n- fly

My refuge is the God of love, My foes insult and cry.   Fly like a tim'rous, trembling dove, Fly &c   To distant mountaine fly

Since I have plac'd my trust in God, A refuge always nigh. Why shou'd I like a tim'rous bird. Why&c To distant mountains fly? Why &c

My trust in God. A refuge &c.   Why should &c.   a tim'rous bird. To distant mountains fly?

A refuge always nigh.   Why should, &c   Why should I like &c.

my trust in God,&c.   Why should, &c.   A tim'rous bird, &c.

My soul come meditate the day And think how near it stands; When thou must quit this house of clay, And fly to unknown lands & fly to

Continued

SAVANNAH. P. M. 8's. Flat Key on C.

unknown &c. O lovely appearance of death, No sight upon earth is so fair. Can with a dead body compare.

Not all the gay pageants that breathe,

SYLVIA. L M. Flat Key on A.

Let music roll in mournful strains,
While death his pris'ners binds in chains;

Bach harper dress'd in grief's attire.
While sorrow tunes her mournful lyre.

Awake. awake each

SYLVIA Continued

Awake. awake.each silent string.
With doleful notes new sorrows bring;

Till forc'd by grief my spirit flies
To the dark shades where Sylvia lies.

TRUMBLE. C M. Flat Key on A.

The promise of my Father's love

LIBERTY. L. M. Sharp Key on F.

'INVITATION LM   Sharp Key on D.

Hark! the redeemer, from on high Gently invites his fav'rites nigh, From caves of darkness, & of doubt, He greatly speaks, & calls us out.

Fly like,

Come my beloved, haste away, Cut short the hours of thy delay; Fly like a youthful hart or roe Over the hills where spices grow.

PART III.

SEVERAL ANTHEMS AND ODES OF THE FIRST EMINENCE

TOGETHER WITH

A FEW PIECES NEVER BEFORE PUBLISHED.

ANTHEM FROM LUKE, 2D CHAP.   Sharp Key on G.   *Stephenson.*

Behold I bring you glad tidings, glad tidings of joy, which shall be to all people.

Behold I bring, &c.

For unto you, unto you is born this day, In the city of David, In &c.

A Saviour who is Christ the Lord.

For unto you, unto you is born this day In &c.

Glad tidings, glad tidings of joy, glad tidings

A saviour who is Christ the Lord Glad tidings, Glad tidings, Glad tidings of joy.

Glad tidings Glad tidings of joy.

which shall be to all people.

You shall find the babe wrapt in swadling cloths, lying

And this shall be a si - - gn u - nto you,

And suddenly there was with the angel a multitude of the heav'n - - - ly

in a manger. ing. &c.

And, &c.

Slow

lost

Glory to God in the highest, Glory, &c.

Prai - - - - - - - - - sing God and saying, Glory to God &c.

and on earth peace peace good will towards men.   Halleujah,   :||:   :||:   :||:   :||:

Halleluj h hallelujah, &c

hands, & they cease not day nor night saying Holy, holy, holy, holy, Lord God Almighty, Which was & is & is to come, Which was & is &

O

is to come.   And I heard a mighty angel fly - ing thro' the midst of heav'n, crying with a loud voice wo, wo, we,

The Lord is risen indeed! ! Hallelujah! The Lord is risen indeed! Halle - lu - jah!

The first fruits of them that slept

Now is Christ risen from the dead, And become the first fruits of them that slept Now is Christ &c.

And did he rise? And did he rise?

Halle'ujah, Hallelujah, Halle - lujah, And did he rise? And did he rise? Did he rise? Hear it ye

nations, hear it, O ye dead! He rose, :||: :||: :||: He burst the bars of death! He burst the bars of death! And triumph'd o'er the grave!

123

Then, :‖: then I rose, :‖: :‖: :‖: then first humanity triumphant past the crystal ports of light, And seiz'd eternal

youth. Man th' immortal hail, hail, Heaven all lavish, of strange gifts to man, Thine all the glory, man's the boundless bliss. Thine &c.

HEAVENLY VISION. Sharp Key on C.

French.

Thousands of thousands & ten times thousands

I beheld and lo a great multitude, which no man could number, Thousands of thousands and ten times thousands, Thousands, &c.

Thousands of thousands and ten times thousands, Thousands &c.

Stood before the Lamb, and they had palms in their

125

wo, be unto the earth by reason of the trumpet which is to sound. And when the last trumpet sounded, the great men & nobles

rich men & poor, bond& free, gathered themselves together, &cried to the rocks &mountains to fall upon them, &hide them from the face of

him that sitsith

DENMARK. Sharp Key on D. [Madan.]

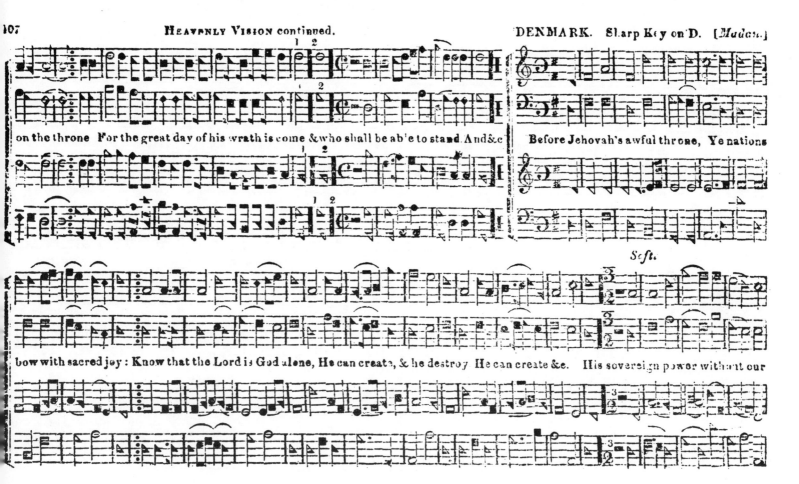

on the throne. For the great day of his wrath is come & who shall be able to stand. And &c

Before Jehovah's awful throne, Ye nations

Soft.

bow with sacred joy: Know that the Lord is God alone, He can create, & he destroy He can create &c.   His sovereign power without our

DENMARK continued.

aid, Made us of clay, & form'd us men, And when like wand'ring sheep we stray'd, He bro't us to his fold again. He &c. We'll crowd thy gates

with

thankful songs, High as the heav'ns our voices raise, And earth, :‖: with her ten thous'nd thous'nd tongues, Shall fill thy courts with soun-

ding praise Shall, &c.

sounding praise. Shall fill, Shall fill, &c. Wide, Wide as the world is thy command, Vast as eternity, eternity, thy love: Firm as a rock thy

Soft.

truth must stand, When rolling years shall cease to move, shall cease to move. When rolling years shall cease to move. When, &c.

JUDGMENT ANTHEM. Flat Key on E.

Morgan

Hark, ye mortals, hear the trumpet, Sounding loud the mighty roar,

Hark! hark!

Hark, the archangel's voice proclaiming Then od time shall be no more

Sounding loud the mighty roar.

See the purple banner flying.

His loud trumpet, his loud trumpet,

Hear the judgment chariot ro - - - - -

rends the tombs, ye dead awake.

ro - ll   breaks thro' yonder cloud,

roll. Hear the sound of Christ victorious, Lo he   Midst ten thousand :||: :||:

Slow   *Lively.*

See he rises thro' the air Hail him :

:||: saints&angels see the crucifyed shine Is that he who died on calv'ry, That was pierced with the spear, tell us seraphs, you that wonder'd,

JUDGMENT ANTHEM continued.

Very lively.

Hail him ; Oh, hail him. Oh yes 'tis Jesus ; Hallelujah, hallelujah, hallelujah, Oh yes 'tis Jesus, O come quickly, O come quickly Oh,

Slow & Grave.

Oh, Come quickly, Hallelujah, Come Lord come Happy, happy, mourners happy mourners, happy mourners, Lo in clouds he

comes he come. Now determin'd ev'ry evil to destroy. All ye nations now shall sing him songs of everlasting joy: Now redemption long expected

View him smiling,

P

See the solemn pomp appear. All his people once rejected, Now shall meet in the air; Hallelujah, ‖: welcome, welcome, bleeding Lamb.

Now his merit

JUDGMENT ANTHEM Continued.

by the harpers, Tho' th' eternal deep resounds, Now resplendant shine his nail prints, Ev'ry eye shall see the wound. They who pierc'd him shall

at his appearance wa - il.

wa - - - il

Ev'ry Island, sea & mountain, heav'n & earth shall flee away; All who hate him must ashamed, Hear the trump proclaim the day,

pierc'd him shall &c.

Come to judgment, :||: :||: Stand before the son of man, Hark, :||: the archangel swells the solemn summon loud. { Tears the strong pil -
{ Hark the shrill out -

lars of the vaults of heaven, Breaks up old marble the repose of princes ; See the graves open and the bones arising, Flames ail around them.
cries of the guilty wretches, Lively bright horror & amazing anguish, stares tho' their eyelids, while the living worm lies gnawing within them.

See the judge's hand arising, Fill'd with vengance on his foes,

Down to hell there's no redemption, Ev'ry Christless soul must go,   Down to hell, depart :||: :||: ye cursed into everlasting flames.

Very slow & soft.   *Brisk*   *Lively & loud.*

Hear the saviour's words of mercy, Come ye ransom'd sinners home ; Swift and joyful in your journey to the palace of your God.

See the souls that earth despised in celes-
Joy celetial hymns harmonious in soft

lestial glories move; Hallelujah big with wonder, Praising Christ's eternal love ; Hallelujah, hallelujah echo through the realms of light.
symphony resound Angels, seraphs harps, & trumpets, Swell the sweet angelic sound; Hail Almighty,   :||:   , Great eternal Lord Amen.

ROSE OF SHARON. Sharp Key on A.   *W. Billings*

I am the rose Sharon and the lilly of the vally

I am the rose of Sharon &c.   As the lilly among the thorns, so

is my love among the daughters. As the apple tree, the apple tree amo - - ng the tree - - s of the wood, So is my beloved among the sons,

I sat down &c.

And his fru - - - it was sweet to my taste.

So is my beloved among the sons,

I sat down under his shadow with great delight

I sat down under &c.

And his fruit, and his fruit was sweet to my taste.

138

And his fruit, & his fruit was sweet to my taste. He brought me to the banquiting house, his banner over me was love. He bro't me to the &c.

And his fru - - it was sweet to my taste-

Stay me with flagons, for I am sick,

banner over me was love. for I am si - - - ck of love.

Comfort me with apples for I am sick

I charge you, O ye daughters of jerusalem, by the roes & by the hinds of the field,   that you stir not up,

that you stir not up,

that you stir not up,

the voice of my beloved,

that you stir not up nor a - wake a - wake a - wake a - wake my love till he please.   Behold! he cometh,

skipping   leaping upon &c   and said unto me.

skipping, leaping upon the mountains, skipping upon the hills.

skipping   leaping upon &c

Q

leaping upon the mountains, skipping   leaping upon &c.   My beloved spake,

rise up,   rise up, my love, my fair one, and come away,   For   lo, the winter is past, the rain is over and gone.   I'or

rise up,

the winter is past, the rain &c.   the rain is over, the rain is over the rain is over and gone. For lo, the winter is past the rain &c

FAREWELL ANTHEM Flat Key on A.

I am going a long and tedious journey never

My friends I am going a long and tedious journey, never to return;   I am going I am going a long and tedious journey, Never

My friends I am &c.   I am going a long journey never to return. I am going a long journey, Never

in that world above, Where trouble shall cease, and harmoney abound.   hark! hark, my dear friends, for death hath called me, And I must

go & lie down in the cold & silent tomb, where the mourners cease from mourning & the pris'ner is set free, Where the rich & the poor are

both alike

Fare you well, :‖: :‖: :‖: Fare you well my friend. Hark ! hark, glad tidings charm our ears, Angelic music fills the

spheres, Earth spreads the sound with distant mirth, A God, A God is born on earth. A God is born the vallies cry, A God is born the hills re-

ply: Ev' ning repeats to won' dring morn, A God, on earth is born. Our frailties long he deig'nd to share, the hier of heav'n of pain the heir; By

miracles his power he tri'd, Preach'd, fasted, sigh'd, & groan'd and dy'd. He liv'd that men might live in peace, He dy'd that sin & death mi't

cease, He rose to prove to hell's fierce pow'rs. Blest immortality is ours.　　　O may we strive like him to live, Our friends estee - m, our

lo.s tongue. Our country love, Our country love,　　　our God adore, Till death and sin shall　reign　no　more.

DAVID's LAMENTATION flat Key on A.

W. Billings

David the king was grieved and moved; he went to his chamber, his chamber and wept; And as he went, he wept, and,

said, O my son! O my son! Would to God I had di'd, would to God I had di'd, would to God I had di'd for thee, O Absalom my son my son.

I heard a great voice from heav'n, saying unto me, write, from hence forth, write, &c write &c blessed are the dead which die in the

Lord

R

Yea saith the spirit for they rest, for they rest, :||: :||: From their labours, :||: from their labours & their works which do

FUNERAL ANTHEM, Continued. PRODIGAL SON, Flat Key on C. *Josiah Moore.*

follow, follow, follow, which do follow, follow them. Which do follow them. Behold! behold the wretch, whose lust and wine Has wasted

his estate; He begs a share amongst the swine, To taste the husks they eat! I die with hunger here, he cries; I starve in foreign lands; My

And &c.

father's house hath large supplies, And bounteous are his hands. I'll go and with a mournful tongue Fall down before his face; Father I've

done thy justice wrong. Nor can deserve thy grace. He said, and hasten'd to his home, To seek his father's love; The father saw the rebel

And all his bowels move. He ran, and fell upon his neck, Embrac'd and kiss'd his son; The reble's heart with sorrow brake, For follies he had

done.

Take of his clothes of shame and sin, The father gives command, Dress him in garments white and clean, With rings adorn his hands

A day of feasting l or-

The LOVER'S LAMENTATION. C. M Flat Key on A.

A. Davisson.

dain, A day of feasting I ordain; Let mirth and joy, :|: abound ; My son was dead, and lives again, Was lost and now is found. Was lost, &c.

Thou lovely chief of all

That awful day will surely come, Th' appointed hour makes haste, When I must stand before the Judge And pass the solemn test

my joys, Thou sov'reign of my heart, How could I bear to hear thy voice Pronounce   The thunder of that dismal word Would so torment my

the sound, "Depart?"   ear,

'Twould tear my soul asunder, Lord, With most tormenting fear. What, to be bannish'd from thy face, And yet forbid to die! To linger in eter-

nal pain,

Yet death forever fly ! O! wretched state of deep dispair, To see my God remove, And fix my doleful station where I must not taste his love.

BUNKERS - HILL AN ODE Flat Key on A.

Why should vain mortals tremble at the sight of Death & destruction Where blood & carnage, :||: clothe the ground in crimson, sounding w

in the field of battle   death groans

155

ODE ON SCIENCE Sharp Key on G.

The morning sun shines from the east, And spreads his glories to the west; All nations with his beams are bless'd Where'e're the radient light appears.

So science spreads her lucid ray, O'er lands which once in darkness lay; She visits fair columbia, And sets her sons among the stares.

Fair freedom her attendant waits, To bless the portals of her gates, To crown the young and rising states With laurels of immortal day.

The British yoke, the gallic chain, Was urg'd upon our necks in vain, All haughty tyrants we disdain, And shout long live America.

MOUNT - CALVARY. 8 8 8 & 6 Flat Key on A.

A. Daviss

The Son of man they did betray, He was condemn'd & led away ; Think, O my soul, that mournful day, Look on Mount Calvary ; Behold him

lamb-like led along, Surrounded by a wicked throng, Accused by each lying tongue, And thus the Lamb of God was hung, Upon the shameful

tree.

☞ Nothwithstanding great pains has be taken to avoid errors, yet some may have escaped notice ; should any be discovered they will be particularly attended to in the next addition : Without further remarks we commit this Work to the hands of a candid, generous, and enlighted public ; believing that a perfect work will not be expected from the hands of man, they are left to judge whether this compilation merits attention or not.